SAVING SCOTTISH FOOTBALL

What we need to do next

By Paul Goodwin

With photos by Stuart Roy Clarke

◆ Tangent Books

First published 2012 by Tangent Books
Unit 5.16 Paintworks,
Arnos Vale,
Bristol, BS4 3EH
0117 972 0645
www.tangentbooks.co.uk
email Richard@tangentbooks.co.uk

ISBN 9781906477820

Copyright Paul Goodwin, Tangent Books
Design: Joe Burt joe@wildsparkdesign.com

A CIP catalogue record for this book is available from the British Library

Printed in Scotland on paper certified as being from sustainable sources by Montgomery Litho Group.

Image credits: Our thanks go to Stuart Roy Clarke at the Homes of football for kindly donating the images for this book.
Front Cover Photo: East Stirlingshire - Fans brave winter at Firs Park© Stuart Roy Clarke

AUTHORS' NOTES
Paul Goodwin

They say that a week is a long time in politics and I believe that football in Scotland exceeded this claim from February until the start of the season in August 2012. In fact Scottish Football could have changed the expression to be *a day is a long time in Scottish Football*. As the Rangers crisis unfolded before our eyes a unique story evolved. It became clear with every passing day that it would have a major impact throughout the whole of the Scottish game. We were brought daily revelations, claims, counter claims, lies, deceit, mystery, intrigue, a heady mix of football politics and of course towards the start of the season football, a fans revolution. So not much to write about then! I had started this book just before the most bizarre period in football started and it was written as those events unfolded. It was not the intention to write as a response to the crisis rather that I already saw the need to change. I just felt unless we did so soon, there would not be much left of our game to save. To me the Rangers implosion brought the crisis to a head in spectacular fashion and suddenly the fans had a voice.

This book is a labour of love and could not have been written without the important contributions of the ex-players, managers administrators and coaches who freely gave their time and agreed to contribute. In buying this book you will be delighted to hear that ALL profits will go to Prostate Cancer Scotland who do a fantastic job in raising awareness and funds to fight a disease that claims 10,000 men's lives every year in the UK . So thank you for your donation to fight this disease.

I would like to thank you for picking this book up and would encourage you to be part of the debate on the future of Scottish Football. Since I started the book I have had an interesting journey which led to my appointment as Head of Supporters Direct Scotland where my brief is to try to represent fans across Scotland, to ensure their views are heard at Government and by the football authorities. I am proud to accept this challenge and to help get ordinary fans the voice that has been so sadly lacking at the top of the game. I do have to say that this is my own personal contribution and not the views of the organisation.

In this new role I remind myself of what Jock Stein said, "Football without fans is nothing, you could have the greatest game in the world; but if there is no people there to watch it means nothing. The fans are the lifeblood of the game". I don't know when or where Jock said it but I do know that the quote is even more valid today than it was 40 years ago.

I would therefore encourage you to be part of the real debates that are happening about OUR game. Please visit the web site www.scottishfans.org to be involved in helping us shape the game or email me at paul@scottishfans.org to be kept up to date with our campaigns.

Special thanks to Scott Grant for his transcriptions and Graeme Young for his editing skill and Richard Jones and his team at Tangent Books. I also appreciated the time Chris Kane gave to facilitating the Focus Groups and his proof reading. Thanks also to Livingston FC and Cumbernauld College for hosting our focus groups and to Rt. Hon Henry McLeish for his on going support of the fans cause and to Jonathan Kennedy of Wave PR. I also have to thank Alex Smith MBE, President of the Scottish League Managers Association for his support with this book. I have to sign off with special thanks to my wife Lynne and kids Gregor and Beth for not complaining too much when I seemed to prefer having my head in a laptop on summer holiday rather than doing other family things. I promise it is the last book ... until the next one that is!

So let's Save Scottish Football......

Paul Goodwin
2012

CHAPTERS

1 INTRODUCTION – ARMAGEDDON OR A LAND OF OPPORTUNITY

The McLeish Report was billed as a watershed moment in Scottish Football. Former East Fife footballer and First Minister, Henry McLeish, produced an in-depth report that looked at how the game in Scotland was governed. It also looked at the performance, or lack thereof, within the national game against the backdrop of a continued lack of progress on the international stage. In short we have been going backwards at both club and international level and this report was designed to be the wakeup call that Scottish Football needed.

The report had an immediate impact and we have already seen the improvements being made by Stewart Regan at the SFA in driving through many of these important structural reforms. Unfortunately, many aspects of the game that the McLeish Report highlighted have not as yet been implemented and that will probably surprise nobody given the various chains of command that are in operation at Hampden Park. When I started writing this book in February 2012, the big issues such as financial fair play and league reconstruction were so far off the radar that it looked like the game was almost paying lip service to them. As I write this we can't escape the fact that we have now witnessed the biggest car crash that has ever taken place in Scottish football. For those who might have been living on another planet, this is also known as the Rangers saga. If you thought that the Star Wars film franchise was a bit contrived, long and far too complicated for its own good then goodness knows what you thought of the Ibrox fiasco. I suppose the only other similarity is that those who ran both these franchises will not complain about the money they made out of them! The only good thing to emerge so far is that this mess has thankfully brought these vital issues to the very top of the agenda and not before time. By the time you read this book many of the day to day issues will have been resolved and the summer pantomime that has been known at Rangers FC will hopefully never be seen again. Of course how we get through this in the long term remains to be seen.

Let's not kid ourselves; the Rangers crisis that has engulfed Scottish Football throughout 2012 has brought its very own tsunami that has wiped away so much of our treasured football history. More than once the word Armageddon was used to describe what was perceived to be just around the corner. However, there is a tangible opportunity to see the big picture and to act in the long term best interests of the game.

It is just a shame that it took such events to stimulate some action and for the voice of the fans to be heard. What has been evident in the aftermath is the fans have delivered a message loud and clear that they want and need integrity in the national game and they want those who run our clubs and our football bodies to listen. The outcome might have been so very different if it had not happened during the close season. Instead we saw the threat of losing season ticket sales held like a gun very firmly against the head of club chairmen across the length and breadth of the country. Did they listen to fans this time - you bet they did!

As far as the McLeish report was concerned, many important issues were not even discussed in this report and concerns such as the decline of football as a spectator and participator sport in our country, the drop in attendances, the lack of atmosphere at games, the pricing policy and how customers were treated in general were sadly lacking in any depth. You cannot blame Henry McLeish who produced a significant amount of work based on what he was asked to look at. This is not a dig at the report, which given how much had gone wrong in the past 40 years, provided a great starting point for the facilitation of change.

The purpose of this book is to try and look at some of these problems and see if we can turn these problems into marketing opportunities. This book has been written between February and early October 2012. This period of time has probably seen the biggest turmoil in our game in 100 plus years. Many of the issues above have seemed to have paled into insignificance with the meltdown of Rangers Football Club. What this backdrop of doom, gloom, litigation, boardroom secrets and financial meltdown has gone to show is that no one Club is bigger than the rest. Now more than ever the thistle must be grasped to ensure financial fair play and integrity is common place and not just wishful thinking. Then and only then can we look to a brighter future where the views of the fans (the customers) are deemed to be as important to the football authorities and the clubs.

2 CONTRIBUTOR PROFILES

Jocky Scott

Jocky Scott was born on the 14th of January 1948 and has spent the majority of his professional career playing and managing in Scotland. Jocky is probably best known for playing with Chelsea, Aberdeen and Dundee and subsequently his three spells as manager at Dundee where he is regarded as a club legend.

Scott, also enjoyed managerial success at Aberdeen, where he was in joint charge of first team duties with Alex Smith from 1988 to 1991. Scott was able to deliver a League Cup and Scottish Cup triumph during his three year spell as co-manager.

This expert of the Scottish game also managed to fit in a short spell playing in America with the Seattle Sounders during the formative years of the North American Soccer League (NASL).

Jocky is held in high esteem in managerial circles and alongside trusted assistant John Blackley, he was in charge at Stirling Albion from January of 2011 until December of the same year.

Jocky has demonstrated his no nonsense approach in the past when speaking about something he feels passionate about. Jocky believes institutional ageism is a problem within the Scottish game and that had a detrimental impact while he was looking for work between leaving Plymouth Argyle in 2005 and eventually returning to Dundee as manager in 2008. In September 2012 he was appointed as the First Team coach at Aberdeen where he teamed up with Craig Brown and Archie Knox in what is the most experienced management team in British football.

CAREER STATS

as a player
393 games
143 goals
2 Scotland caps

as a manager
Managed 11 clubs Scotland &England
currently First Team coach Aberdeen

Alex Smith MBE

Alex Smith is a Scottish football legend. Alex has been involved with the game in Scotland since singing for Kilmarnock in 1958 and then making his debut as a teenager with Stenhousemuir in 1959. In the 53 years that have followed Alex has managed to pick up a wealth of experience which is up there with the elite names in the sport.

Alex has enjoyed an almost uninterrupted run during his playing and managerial career. Smith made his name as an inside striker around Central Scotland. Alex enjoyed spells with the aforementioned Stenhousemuir before joining his local club Stirling Albion. Those spells were followed with short stints at East Stirlingshire and Albion Rovers before finishing his playing career back where it all began with Stenhousemuir.

Alex's managerial career began before his playing career had ended. Before he retired with the *Warriors* in 1970 he had already taken the reins at Ochilview Park. Alex was in charge of Stenhousemuir for six years before returning to Stirling Albion where he spent twelve years in charge. A two-year spell with St Mirren followed with a Scottish cup win. Alex then spent three years in co-charge with fellow contributor Jocky Scott at Aberdeen. Alex had another season in sole charge in 1991-92.

Alex followed that up with a two-year spell at Clyde before taking over the reins of the Scottish Under 21 side. Alex has been lauded throughout his stellar career for his determination to always give youth a chance. He went on to spend two seasons in charge at Dundee Utd at the turn of the millennium.

Alex followed that up with a spell in the Highlands with Dingwall based Ross County, where he managed between 2002 to 2005.

Perhaps one of his most rewarding jobs has come at the twilight of his career. Alex joined up with rising manager Steven Pressley at Falkirk and together they have developed players from the club's highly successful youth academy. Alex is still as passionate about the game as he has ever been and is in his element on the training field teaching young players how they game should be played. He is president of the Scottish League Managers Association; a position he has held for many years and was awarded an MBE for services to football.

CAREER STATS

as a player	as a manager
148 games	Managed 7 clubs sides
24 goals	Scotland U21

Brian Rice

Brian Rice is a tremendously popular player and coach who spent a considerable time of his career in the English top flight with Brian Clough's Nottingham Forest.

Before his move to England, Brian got his break at Hibernian, where he spent several seasons honing his craft before his big move.

A cult hero at Forest, Brian despite the act he only made just over 90 appearance for a side which won two league cups during his six year spell at the club.

Brian was revered by the City Ground faithful during his time at the club and still retains a cult following, with yellow submarine based 'A team of Brian Rice's' still a firm favourite sing song at matches.

After a loan spell with Stoke City, Brian returned to the Scottish game with Falkirk. Brian would make over 100 league appearances during his time at Brockville.

Brian would then go and make over 50 appearances for Clyde before joining Ian McCall at Greenock Morton as assistant manager. He would then follow McCall to Airdrieonians but after the club ceased to exist they found themselves at Falkirk. Brian would decide to stay on at the club after McCall moved on to Dundee Utd, Brian would forge a good working relationship with manager John Hughes. The pair would eventually leave Falkirk for Brian's first club Hibs. Where they would spend a year and a half in charge. Brian is now coaching in the Middle East.

CAREER STATS
as a player
362 games
30 goals

Sandy Clark

Sandy Clark was born on the 28th of October 1956 and has forged a well-respected career in the media as a pundit and co-commentator alongside an impressive playing and managerial career.

Airdrie born Clark made his name with his hometown club where he spent eight seasons. Sandy made over 200 league appearances for *The Diamonds* in which he scored 92 goals for the club. Sandy was named the *PFA Players' Player of the Year* in 1982.

His impressive form for Airdrie didn't go unnoticed and he ended up making a move to English first division side West Ham United. Sandy made 26 league appearances for *The Hammers* before returning to Scotland with Rangers the following season.

Sandy joined Hearts in 1986 and went on to make over 150 appearances for the club and was one of the club's key players when the club narrowly missed out on securing the league title in the 1985-86 season.

After leaving the Gorgie side, Sandy took charge at Partick Thistle in a player-manager role. He spent a year at Firhill before having a short spell playing with Dunfermline Athletic.

Sandy would go on to manage Hearts and Hamilton Academicals before taking charge at St Johnstone. He led *The Saints* to a remarkable third place finish in the 1998/99 season and into Europe.

Sandy went on to manage Berwick Rangers in 2004 but he is probably best known to a younger audience as a co-commentator on BBC's football coverage during the early-mid 2000's. Sandy alongside Rob McLean were the broadcasters flagship duo and their rapport was a staple of the coverage.

Sandy is currently the assistant manager at Queen of the South where he works alongside manager Allan Johnston, who he managed while he was at Hearts. He has the pleasure of working with Nicky his son who is he Queen's centre forward.

CAREER STATS

as a player	as a manager
465 games	Managed 5 clubs
155 goals	currently Assistant Manager Queen of the South

Jackie McNamara

Jackie McNamara, the son of legendary Hibs player Jackie Snr, began his distinguished footballing career at Dunfermline Athletic. His eye-catching performances alerted then Celtic manager Tommy Burns and he moved to the side his father began his career with in 1995.

Jackie didn't take long to settle in Glasgow and soon established himself in the first team. One of the highlights during the 1995/96 season for Hoops fans was the link-up play between Jackie at right back and midfielder Simon Donnelly. Jackie would go on to claim the *Scottish PFA Young Player of the Year* at the end of that season.

McNamara continued his impressive displays at Celtic under managers Wim Jansen and Dr. Josef Venglos. His form also never wavered even during the poor 1999/2000 campaign which was overseen by Kenny Dalglish and John Barnes.

When Martin O'Neill arrived in the summer of 2000, Celtic's fortunes changed on the pitch. While Jackie wasn't a regular in the early stages of the Northern Irish manager's tenure, he proved to be a key player for a Celtic side which reached the UEFA Cup final in Seville at the end of 2002/03 season. McNamara would also go on to be capped 33 times for the Scottish national team.

McNamara's final game in Green and White was his testimonial against the Republic of Ireland. McNamara would then make the move to England where he would spend two seasons at Molineux with Wolverhampton Wanderers.

Jackie would return to Scotland in 2007 with Aberdeen. A two-year spell at Falkirk followed before he moved on loan to Partick Thistle. He made the move permanent for 2010/11 campaign and before the season was out he was put in caretaker charge following the departure of manager Ian McCall.

McNamara began the job on a full-time basis ahead of the 2011/12 campaign and he would lead *The Jags* to a respectable sixth placed finish in the always competitive Scottish First Division. His close friend Simon Donnelly is his number two at Thistle, who proudly sit at the top of the First Division after the first quarter of the season.

CAREER STATS

as a player	**as a manager**
421 games	Managed Partick Thistle (current)
13 goals	
33 Scotland caps	

David MacKinnon

David Donaldson MacKinnon (born 23 May 1956 in Glasgow) is a Scottish former professional football player who is best known for his time as a Football Club Executive as much as a player

David left his home in Renfrew as a youngster to sign professional terms with Arsenal. After four years in London without breaking into the first team he came back to Scotland to play for Dundee. A move closer to home saw him join Bertie Auld's Partick Thistle in the SPL Whilst at Thistle he won a Scottish League Cap against Northern Ireland in 1980.

He joined Rangers from Partick Thistle for £30,000 in May 1982 having overcome a major serious injury that led to the loss of a kidney aged 24.

Dave was a wholehearted defender who had pace and was very much an attacking full back so common in the modern game where they are deployed as wing backs. MacKinnon departed Ibrox after the arrival of Graeme Souness, moving to Airdrie in 1986. He scored the Division 2 promotion clinching penalty kick for Kilmarnock against Cowdenbeath on the final day of the 1989-90 season. He finished his career at Forfar Athletic and started working for Tennent's- Scotland's leading brewer and then as Operations Director of Scotland's largest independent pub retailer.

Following the sale of the company in 2002, he took this commercial experience back into football with Clyde and went on to be chief executive at Kilmarnock and latterly Dundee. MacKinnon was also a reporter for Sportsound on BBC Radio Scotland during the late 1990s. David now has his own new management and events company working in projects in the Middle East and China

CAREER STATS
as a player
played 404 games
scored 9 goals

John Blackley

John Blackley was born on the 12th of May 1948 in Westquarter. John began his successful playing career with Hibernian in 1967. He would go on to spend 11 seasons with the club where he made over 250 league appearances.

The silky centre back then moved to England where he enjoyed spells with Newcastle United and Preston North End. He returned to Scotland in 1981 with Hamilton Academicals where he spent two seasons in a player/manager role. John finished his playing career where it began with brief playing spell for Hibernian before taking over as manager in 1984. John was manager at the Easter Road side until 1986.

John would then go on to be Paul Sturrock's long-term assistant manager at a variety of clubs including two spells at Plymouth Argyle, Dundee Utd, St Johnstone, Sheffield Wednesday and Swindon Town.

After he left Plymouth Argyle in the summer of 2009, his next job was with fellow veteran Jocky Scott, who he assisted at Stirling Albion from January to December of 2011.

John's longevity in the game pays testament to his passion for football which he now takes onto the golf course with him in his retirement.

CAREER STATS

as a player	as a manager
416 games	Managed 2 clubs
6 goals	Assistant 8 clubs
7 Scotland caps, including playing in 1974 World Cup Finals	
1 Scottish League Cap	

Kevin McGoldrick

Kevin has forged an excellent career for himself in Scottish Football from his humble beginning as a Queens Park player to become one of our mostly highly regarded youth coaches. He played for Queens Park and moved to East Stirlingshire before a return to Hampden. It was at the national stadium where he made his mark as a gutsy wing back and as a youth was selected for many international youth squads. When his playing career ended he got involved in coaching at Queens Park where his reputation took him to Stenhousemuir. He progressed to become first team coach and the assistant manager under Davie Irons. He continues in that role working alongside Martyn Corrigan and is tipped by many for a bigger job.

CAREER STATS

as a player	as a manager
87 games	Asst Manager (currently with Stenhouesmuir)
6 goals	

Des McKeown

Des McKeown is one of the most respected figures in Scottish Football due to his playing career, work within the media and his role with the Scottish Football Association.

Des enjoyed an impressive playing career. He began his career in the Celtic youth team before spells with Airdrieonians, Albion Rovers, Partick Thistle and Stenhousemuir. He enjoyed two successful spells at Queen of the South. He was part of *The Doonhamers* side which reached the 1997 Challenge Cup final.

In 2001, Des was the subject of a book written by journalist Bill Leckie. The book which was entitled "Don't Give Up the Day Job: A Year in the Life of a Part-Time Footballer". The book looked at how Des managed to balance his part-time footballing career with his role working in office supplies and balancing family life.

After suffering a broken leg, which effectively ended his playing career, Des spent two seasons in charge at Stenhousemuir. In the first season he was co-manager with Tony Smith before taking full control ahead of the 2005/06 campaign.

Since leaving Ochilview, McKeown has forged quite the career within the Scottish media. McKeown regularly contributes to BBC football programmes and he also has his own weekly column in The Sun newspaper. Des has proven to be a successful pundit due to his likeable nature and the wealth of experience he has gathered about the Scottish game.

Des is now in charge of his own Office Supplies company and he also provides match analysis for Scotland's National Team as well as running marathons for charity.

CAREER STATS

as a player	**as a manager**
458 games	Managed Stenhousemuir in Scotland
3 goals	

Darren Jackson

Jackson has the rather unique distinction of having started and ended his career in Scottish football with teams that are no longer playing in senior football. He began his career in 1985 with Meadowbank Thistle and he finished at Clydebank. At Meadowbank his impressive performances won him a move to Newcastle United. He spent two years with the Magpies, and returned to Scotland in 1988 with a highflying Dundee United. Jackson spent four years at Tannadice, picking up a Scottish Cup runners-up medal, before joining hometown team Hibernian in 1992. During his five years at Easter Road, Jackson was a runner-up again, this time in the League Cup and his form saw him move to Celtic in 1997. During his time at Celtic, Jackson was treated for hydrocephalus - water on the brain - requiring surgery in September 1997 although he was soon playing again and Celtic went on to win both the League and League Cup. The following season, Jackson had a spell on loan with Coventry City, before joining his boyhood heroes Hearts.

In October, Jackson was barred from playing for Hearts due to the impending trigger of a clause enforcing a one-year extension to his contract, Jackson negotiated a deal to return to first-team action at Hearts, only to find himself surplus to requirements when Craig Levein was appointed three weeks later.

In January, Jackson joined Livingston on a month's loan, subsequently extending it until the end of the season. where he won the First Division title. Jackson then returned to the Premier League with St Johnstone on a one-year contract. Jackson made nine league appearances for *the Saints* before being allowed to join Clydebank on loan in January 2002, where he scored a début goal in a 1-0 win.

Jackson won 28 caps for Scotland, scoring four goals. Making his début in March 1995, Jackson was also part of the Scotland squads for Euro 96 and the 1998 World Cup, playing in two of the World Cup matches. Jackson played two further games after the tournament, appearing in the European Championship qualifying matches.

Despite Jackson's earlier vow to move into management, he works as one of the SFA's 52 agents representing players including fellow Scots Jackie McNamara, Mark Wilson and Steven Thompson.

CAREER STATS

as a player	as a manager
493 games	28 Scotland caps scoring 4 goals
123 goals	

Steven Tweed

A criticism of many British players is that they are often reluctant to go abroad to further their footballing development, a criticism which cannot be levelled at Steven Tweed. The towering Edinburgh born centre-half enjoyed spells in Greece, Germany, England and Japan during a colourful playing career.

Steven began his career in 1991 with Hibernian and he spent five years with the Easter Road club. Steven then made his first of several trips abroad when he signed for Greek side Ionikos in 1996.

His appearances were limited and he soon returned to British football with Stoke City in 1997.

Steven returned to the Scottish game and spent a three year spell with Dundee. He made over 80 appearances for the club. He was on the move abroad again during the summer of 2001 when he signed for German outfit MSV Duisburg. He spent three years at the club.

What followed was probably the most adventurous period of his career. He made a move to Japan, where he starred for Yokohama FC for two seasons. Tweed was one of the key players in the side and was featured prominently in several team of the year's after the 2005 season.

He made his return to Scotland in the Summer of 2006 and signed for Livingston. He would then move on to East Fife, initially on loan, before signing up at Montrose on a player/manager deal.

Steven would spend over two years with the club before resigning in March 2011. He would go to spend a short period with junior side Broughty Athletic between June and December of last year.

Steven possesses unique insight due to his well-travelled football career and experience within all levels of the Scottish game and will surely re-emerge as a coach or manager again soon.

CAREER STATS

as a player		as a manager
Scotland	260	Managed Montrose
Greece	2	
England	65	
Germany	70	
Japan	120	
Total	*517 games, 17 goals*	

Davie Hay

Davie Hay was born on the 29th of January 1948 in Paisley. Hay would begin his footballing journey at Celtic in 1968 and would go on to play more than 150 games for the team. After a difference in opinion, Hay moved to Chelsea in 1974 after a stunning World Cup campaign where many commentators had him in the team of the tournament even though he only played 3 games. Hay would make 27 appearances for the national team.

Hay suffered several setbacks during his career. He had to retire after a serious knee injury and he also suffered a detached retina, which eventually led to him losing his sight in his right eye.

Hay began his managerial career at Motherwell in 1981 and spent two seasons at the Fir Park club. He would then rejoin Celtic as manager in 1983. In his four years in charge, he secured a league title and Scottish Cup for the club. Hay was challenged for honours as much by the 'New Firm' in the form of Aberdeen and Dundee Utd as he was by traditional rivals Rangers in what was the toughest time ever to be a Celtic manger given the level of competition rarely seen before or since then.

Hay would then go on to have a successful year in Norway with Lillestrom. In his sole year in charge they were crowned league champions for only the fifth time in their history, the club have not won a league title since Hay's departure.

Hay returned to management in Scotland in 1991 as manager of St Mirren where he spent two years in charge. Hay then became a scout with former club Celtic, where he used his extensive knowledge of European football in helping the club acquire targets such as Pierre Van Hooijdonk, Jorge Cadete and Paulo Di Canio.

He then linked up with Jim Leishman at Livingston, initially as General Manager before becoming Co- Manager which again helped the club greatly on the field. He helped lead the club into a third place finish in 2001/02 and most memorably in season 2003-4 delivered the club its finest moment by beating Hibernian 2-0 to lift the Scottish League Cup.

Hay would go on to have a season in charge at Dunfermline Athletic during the 2004/05 season and after returning to Livingston in an advisory role he was in the dug out for the final few matches of the season 2005/6 when he saved the Lions from what weeks before many thought was almost certain relegation.

David is one of the he most knowledgeable men in Scottish football and his connections within the game in Europe make him a man you listen to when he speaks about the game.

CAREER STATS

as a player	as a manager	International caps
316 games	Managed 7 clubs	27 Scotland caps
13 goals		

Jimmy Calderwood

James "Jimmy" Calderwood (born 28 February 1955 in Glasgow) was most recently the manager of Go Ahead Eagles. Calderwood played for English club Birmingham City where his boss was England World Cup winner Sir Alf Ramsey. He also played at Cambridge

United (on loan) and Dutch clubs Sparta Rotterdam, Willem II Tilburg, Roda JC and Heracles Almelo. After retiring as a player, Calderwood stayed in the Netherlands and became a coach, becoming a manager of Willem II Tilburg and NEC Nijmegen.

He returned to his native Scotland in 1999 to become manager of Dunfermline Athletic, guiding them to the 2004 Scottish Cup Final. Calderwood left Dunfermline that summer to become manager of Aberdeen, a position he held for five seasons. Aberdeen performed well in the SPL under Calderwood and reached the last 32 of the 2007–08 UEFA Cup, but suffered a number of domestic cup defeats by lower league opponents. He then had brief stints with Kilmarnock and Ross County, helping each club retain their league status. Calderwood returned to the Netherlands in March 2012, with Go Ahead Eagles and is currently looking for a position abroad.

CAREER STATS

as a player	**as a manager**
316 games	Managed 7 clubs in Holland & Scotland
13 goals	

Jamie McGowan

Jamie learned his trade as a defender with his home town club Morecambe before a move to Dundee in 1992. However it was with his next club, Falkirk, that Jamie made his mark; 131 appearances, 8 of his 14 career goals, club captain and leading his team out at Hampden in the 1997 Scottish Cup final and 1998 Scottish Cup semi final. In 1998 Jamie moved to Motherwell for the inaugural SPL season where he stayed two years.   After moves to St Mirren, Alloa and Albion Rovers, Jamie officially retired at East Fife in 2008. Today, Jamie runs his own business in Falkirk where he lives with his wife and daughters, and is an occasional media pundit for the Bairns.

CAREER STATS
as a player
Played 316
12 goals

3 THE ROAD TO CHANGE

The Smith Museum in Stirling is the starting point for this little book and my quest to find some innovative solutions to help save Scottish football from its seemingly inevitable slide into total obscurity.

Let me explain, it's December 2011 on a freezing cold winters day just six days before Christmas and I am at the press launch of 'Saving the Albion', the wee book that Tom Bowser and myself wrote to commemorate the purchase of Stirling Albion Football Club, as the first fans owned senior club in Scotland. The last thing on my mind today is thinking about writing another book and being wedded to my laptop for another 6 months or so!

As part of that memorable campaign, I saw the value in using the fact that the oldest football in the world had been ensconced in this tiny museum in Central Scotland. I used "the ba" to help drive the PR message that the fight to save Stirling Albion was really important, not just to Binos fans; but to the wider football world. I tried to do this by reinforcing the message that the city of Stirling was in fact the birthplace of modern world football. It is quite a claim but here is the story for those of you who missed it last time around. Get ready to go back in time for our unique trip down *futebal* history.

The ball was discovered some 20 years ago. It is made from Cow hide with a Pig's bladder used to inflate the ball. It is just about half the size of the Adidas Tango 12 that was used at the Euro Championships in Poland and Ukraine. The world's oldest football was made in Stirling by a local craftsmen long before the Germans and Americans at Adidas and Nike had any idea what football was all about. It came as quite a shock that during renovations of the Queen's Chamber in Stirling Castle, which was decorated in the 1540's, this wee ba' was discovered behind the wood and plaster panelling. So did Mary, Queen of Scots invent football? Well it is impossible to say; but it is could just be true as she would certainly have seen it played in her times.

It is known that Mary, Queen of Scots was in residence at this time and later in her life we know she had an interest in all sports; but especially golf and football. She recorded a game of *futebal* in her diaries while at Carlisle Castle. The ball could have been used in the courtyards within the castle or taken to the Royal gardens below the walls to be played in the grounds of Kings Park. Which ironically was the name of the original team that represented Stirling, until Hitler's bombs killed the team off with a direct hit to their Forthbank ground. The local historians (now proud guardians of this world first) tell us that everyone from the castle, including Kings and Queens would have been involved in playing *futebal* as it was a game for all, just as it is today; but what we do know is that this wee ball could indeed have been there at the beginning of a sport that now undoubtedly is the number one sport in the world. From such humble beginnings the wee ba started a revolution and on this day it was going to prompt me to start this book.

On the day of our book launch, while we await the arrival of our photographer, Tom said to me, "Well Mr Creative, Saving the Albion was easy; but with the Scottish game in complete turmoil, I think we could all do with you getting your head round how the hell you save Scottish football?" It is of course a ridiculous proposition. How could it be saved? Is it worth saving? Had the McLeish Report not tried to do the same? What could I bring to the table? Can I play some small part in bringing about some of the necessary changes that could maybe just make a difference? By the time I left the Smith Museum my head was full of ideas. Something did need to be done of that there is no doubt and this book is my contribution to the debate. Another labour of love to keep me out of mischief.

So the seed was sown and the format of the book was developed. The plan would become that I would write a chapter about a topic for change and I would then open that up to a couple of focus groups of industry professionals - the guys who play, manage and coach the game to see if they like or dislike some of the concepts. Of course then I decided to chat to a few other people who I thought might have a view that we should listen to and that I think lead to some interesting viewpoints. Some of the ideas are new, some are just us tackling the topics which have been mooted in the past, such as when and where we play, and other suggestions come from looking at successful aspects of other sports. I was really surprised at that outcome on some of the topics I suggested. Where I expected resistance, such as with the much discussed topic of summer football, we ended up with the professionals fully endorsing the concepts. With some other more radical suggestions I was sent home to think again which doesn't mean they are bad ideas necessarily; but that is the aim of this book, to get people talking.

However, what came through loud and clear was the fans want change and so to do those who are playing, coaching and managing at the highest end of our professional game. So fasten your seat belts and join me as we try to get Scottish Football moving in the right direction again.

4 FOCUS GROUPS AND KEY INDIVIDUALS

To try and get to the bottom of these complex issues I have recruited a range of football professionals who came together to help explore whether these proposed solutions could in fact work or indeed whether, with the insight and knowledge of these professionals, they could be adapted.

The coaches and managers panel made up of most of our focus groups. In addition to this I have also taken council from Bryan Jackson and Donald McGruther who run many clubs between them when they went into administration.

So here we hear their views on why Scottish Football must change if it has any hope of growing or else it will continue to stagnate.

I started with our panel of experts by asking **"what do you see wrong with Scottish Football?"** I asked this question on the basis that once we got the answers it was a good starting point for exploring what the solutions might be.

THE OFF THE FIELD TEAM

Can you give me a summary of what you see wrong with Scottish Football?

Donald McGruther Director of Insolvency, Scotland at Mazars
Without question Scottish Football is in a mess and it has been getting worse year after year. When I stepped in at Falkirk – when it went into Provisional Liquidation - it seemed that the club was run differently than any other type of business. Clubs can't ignore the fact that they should know much money they can afford to spend. It seems obvious don't you think? For me the problems in our game stems from the very top of our game. We have 3 bodies running the game all with vested interests and that is hardly going to lead to moving football forward. I also think that the SPL is a failed experiment and that we need to go back to go forward with better (fairer) distribution of wealth and a much larger league that stimulates competition at all levels of the game. My team are in the SPL and nobody I talk to looks forward to the start of the season the way they used to. The main reason for that is not about the quality of play (which we have to accept is in decline) but the fact we have the same old boring games 4 times a season. It has got to

end soon or we will continue to lose customers forever.

Bryan Jackson partner at PKF

I believe that the main thing wrong with Scottish football has been historically a lack of financial discipline and we have seen a culture where clubs have been spending more than they generate year on year. Being a football fan myself, it is understandable that clubs chase the holy grail but overspending on players cannot be sustained. Also, in the past, there has been a rich benefactor model in the UK in many cases and this again eventually leads to financial difficulties. For example, at Gretna the benefactor died and more recently at Dundee, the benefactor's personal circumstances changed and he was unable to maintain his financial support. Even closer to home, as you know, at Stirling it is hard for a benefactor, aged 83, to convince his family that he should continue to spend the family silver.

I think another problem with Scottish football is the administrative set up and the staleness that has crept into the present league structure. I would like to see those at the top of the administration of the game taking more advice from those that have football and financial experience.

THE FOOTBALL TEAM

Jocky Scott

I guess I played in the golden era of Scottish Football with great players, decent crowds and far more competition in the top league. It just feels as if it is now broken and needs fixed. I firmly believe that the SPL is far too negative and too restrictive to allow decent football to flourish and if you have a poor product on the park then people will not come to watch it. It all starts at the top and we have too many people looking after themselves and not enough heed paid to the knowledge and expertise of football people who know the industry. Funny enough they don't listen to what the fans want either.

John Blackley

I was lucky that I had great managers such as Bob Shankly and Eddie Turnbull who knew football inside out and wanted us to always express ourselves. That led to a better quality of football than what a stagnant league can muster. If you factor in that less kids are playing football and folk have more hobbies in their recreation time then it leads to an overall decline in the quality of what you watch and that means less people want to go to the game. We undoubtedly need change and my generation of traditionalists need to embrace it or there will be no game left for future generations to fall in love with. I see the game in crisis and it worries me. We can't keep talking about it; what we need is action.

Steven Tweed

We need to take the fear factor out of the game for managers and coaches and that will take the fear factor away from the players. If we all want to see better quality football it is pretty simple - better facilities, better coaching and of course having a league structure that works for everybody. I really don't see this as being complicated and I found that in my time playing abroad they were far more open to change. The people at the top have a responsibility to the game and they should not forget that. Having bigger leagues is just the start of it. If it means the clubs have less money then maybe they will give more young local talent a platform. What are they waiting for?

Davie Hay

The fans, players and coaches are the most important thing in the game, in fact you could go as far as saying they are the game. Jock Stein always said it was about those who play and those who pay and the rest doesn't matter. We need to listen to what our supporters, players and managers want and then maybe we will have a chance to change things in a way that will get more people involved in the game. To me football needs to listen if it is to survive.

Kevin McGoldrick

I think all the leagues are too tight and that they should be expanded. Unless you are flying away with the league title you really find it hard to find the space to let teams express themselves. The play-offs do help; but the big picture is that we need better coaching, better players, a more expansive game and more people wanting to come and watch it.

Alex Smith

We need to take a long hard look at the situation. We have already wasted years since the McLeish Report and we need to look at radical solutions rather than tinkering at the edges of what is broken. League reconstruction and summer football are massive issues that need addressed. All the authorities marketing the game together and helping us get a better product on the park is essential too. We need the leadership at the top of the game to take control and to make it happen.

Des McKeown

We all know that the game is not working the way it should. Standards have been dropping in every part of the game whether it be the quality of the product on the park or whether it is in terms of governance in boardrooms up and down the country. We need to start changing now if we want to get our credibility back and start to believe in ourselves. If we don't, I really do fear for the future at all levels of the game.

David Mackinnon

For a start too many people knocking it! In recent years I have been fortunate to have witnessed many superb games played by enthusiastic and skilful players but if you were to believe all you read and hear about our game you would think these games never happen. It's been fashionable in recent years to talk the game down. Sure it needs restructuring and leadership to get back on track but above all it needs passionate and dedicated people running it. Many people currently in the authority in Leagues, Associations or Clubs are in it for what they can get out of it and what it does for their CV. This leads to mistrust in authority by the fans and who can blame them. Weed out the egos and the attention seekers and get more fan groups involved in running clubs and then we'll see the game getting its pride and credibility back.

Jamie McGowan

I still think we have a product that people want; it is just that there are so many other things that football competes against nowadays. When you look at the First Division, my old team Falkirk are doing their bit by bringing through young local talent; but as there is no playoff in the division and you are playing each other four times so it is hard to make it attractive in its current format. The leagues need to wake up to the fact that even die-hard fans can't take it anymore.

Jackie McNamara

We need to start at the top of the game. We need to keep as many full time teams in the game as possible (to develop talent) and we need to make it far more exciting. Let's get rid of the fear factor, make sure there are bigger leagues with more opportunities for the likes of playoffs which mean more teams are in the hunt towards the end of the season. Playing each other four times in a season is dull for managers, for players and I think for fans too. I know we are told all the time that is the way it has to be; but I think we need to challenge that. It was so much better when I played in England with bigger leagues and just playing each other twice. I really hope we get change sooner rather than later as we have a duty to the next generations.

Darren Jackson

I do recognise that there is a need for change in Scottish Football We have made big strides at the grassroots side of the game - my son is at Alloa Athletic and the coaching is good and the kids are all eating and drinking well; but kids should be playing in small sides and pitches up to say 14 years old. That way we would need to develop a passing a game to support it. There are probably too many games against the same opposition so I guess I am saying like everybody else a bigger league is called for.

Jimmy Calderwood

You just need to look at the big picture. In the lower leagues it is far more competitive. It is simple because the sides are evenly matched and are of a similar size and have similar incomes and that is what makes it attractive to fans. We have been calling for change for far too long. We need to look to the Dutch model with the SFA controlling the leagues so we can do away with the infighting and everybody looking out for themselves.

Brian Rice

To me it is really simple. Play more attractive football in bigger leagues with as many local derbies as you can organise. I would also start the ball rolling by playing on the best playing surfaces in the best conditions which means summer football. Radical maybe; but simple. I really don't think you need to be a rocket scientist to sort it out; but the Blazers just keep talking about it rather than doing anything about it. It's shocking.

5 UNDERSTANDING THE FANS

How can we grow if we don't properly know our audience.

There is of course the old adage that you can't flog a dead horse. Without significant structural change, no matter what schemes you offer you will simply not be able to get enough **new** fans through the gates to justify the investment in these areas. So what we have is what businesses call 'customer churn' where you are losing more fans that you are managing to bring in. Given how long it takes to make a fan then you can see that the picture looks gloomy.

For the so called provincial clubs there is a dilemma in that there are football fans within their area who are only attracted to the two big successful clubs: Celtic and Rangers. I am sure that it would not take a major research paper into the psychology of the behaviour of sports fans to get to the bottom of why people want (and need) to follow successful clubs never mind the history of the sectarian and religious issues that have blighted our game. It is important as a matter of research to understand how we become fans and how over the past 20 or 30 years this has changed. Every business worth its salt needs to understand their market and I am sorry to say that this is something that is completely lacking in Scottish Football.

Everything we are told about fans is based on a little knowledge, anecdotal evidence, some previous history and of course the age old navel gazing and its sister, the gut feel. No business in the world would go into such dramatic period of change (as will be happening in October 2012 onward with the discussions on the future of the game) without the detailed knowledge of its customers. Of course there is no evidence to suggest that even if these basic foundations were in place those who control our game would take any notice of what the customers want. But that, as they say, is another story.

So here we want to do things properly and before we talk about the much needed changes in Scottish Football we will start by looking at who the customers are and look to see what opportunities might exist to talk to them.

THE ROUTE TO BEING A FAN

The family

The most common route to becoming a fan is to follow in your father's footsteps and start your journey as part of your family birthright. Of course when you break the link through the aforementioned churn you have far more difficulty in capturing the next generation of fans.

In my own instance my mother's father was from Partick and my father's family were from Scotstoun, both on the banks of the River Clyde. Both my Grandfathers worked in the Clyde Shipyards as Shipwrights and both were proud owners of season books, as they used to be called, for Partick Thistle. So there was never any doubt that as both my Dad and his brother became Jags fans and that it would continue down the line. However even with that happy family connection we can see that over the past 30 years in my family there is a dilution in the loyalty which is a huge change from the previous generation. So many factors coming to play from the change in the community as a whole, to the diminishing importance of football as a part of the fabric of our society, to the many other alterative opportunities that exist to use the leisure time that once was the sole claim of the football industry. In this scenario we can see where football has lost its way.

The location

It is so much easier in larger countries like Spain, France, Germany, Italy and to an extent England too where there are larger population bases to support the league structures. With large cities there is plenty of space for good sized clubs to prosper. In Scotland we just don't have the luxury of having a decent spread of population. What would be ideal is for fans who live in say Falkirk to follow Falkirk the local team. Of course many do; but as we know to the detriment of the game far too many leave their home towns to follow our two other big clubs. As the say - success breeds success. Great for them but bad for the economics of our game. Of course if you are born in Hamilton there is a good chance that you might end up being an Accies fan.

The friend

Quite often a friend will introduce somebody to the game or a club and that introduction will stick whether it is as a second team or indeed at the primary team of choice of the individual. This season my son's pals have been to a few Partick Thistle games with me (kids go free) and some Stirling Albion games (our local club) and I would think if we continue to do so these will become their teams.

The school and the work place

I recall asking Stuart MacPhee the SPL Commercial Manager why he supported his team when we were discussing the unique attributes of being a Partick Thistle fan. Like many fans who had parents who were not major football advocates Stuart found himself at a school where all his pals followed to one degree or another a big team. He didn't like swimming with the tide and decided to follow the opposition. However, the reality is that peer group pressure is likely to take you in one direction or another as conforming is sometimes much easier than Stuart's route.

THE RANDOM REASON

Away from home

It might be a work placement or moving away from home to University or college that ignites a spark. A friend of mine Andrew Jenkin is a West Ham United supporter and all round East End boy. He studied at Stirling University and our paths crossed as we picked up on the Stirling Albion story that was unfolding just along the road from him. Andrew and several of his colleagues decided that helping the Binos would be a good experience for his fledgling career in journalism and within a year they had produced a fantastic magazine for the club. I am sure in years to come they will always have the Binos as their second/Scottish team.

Other unique reasons

We have all heard that Stenhousemuir have a fantastic fans base in Norway. The Norwegian Supporters Club was set up almost 20 years ago and has in excess of 100 members. It is one of the largest foreign supporters clubs outside of the English Premiership.

The Norwegians Supporters Club has sponsored the football club in many ways since their inception and currently sponsors the main stand, now called the Norway Stand. They have also among other things sponsored the Youth Programme and organised a pre-season tour to Norway for the 1st team in recent years.

TYPE OF FANS - BUILDING THE PICTURE

Derived from research from Beech & Chadwick (2004, p137 *"The Business of Sports Management"*). The two authors (particularly Beech who has his own journals of football finance and marketing) outlined the following approaches to marketing to a sports fan. Before we properly look at the ways that we can develop cohesive marketing plans to build our fan base we need to understand our fans and what they mean to both clubs and the league. So just as all good marketing plans start with market research then so we start this section of the book by trying to understand more about the football audience. From this initial work I have developed a more detailed specific audience profile for Scottish Football fans which I am happy for the industry to utilise in the future (I will not be hard to deal with).

CHARACTERISTICS OF A FAN

TEMPORARY: *Interested for a specific time period (e.g. special event, specific sports personality, influence of others), typically impulse or semi-impulse behaviours. For example, a fan that supports the national team at the Olympics or fan that supports golf because Tiger Woods is playing, but will stop when he retires.*

In Scottish terms I know loads of sports fans who followed the career of David Coulthard with interest in the world of F1 yet have never watched a race in quite the same way since he retired. In Scottish Football terms this is the Scottish Cup Final syndrome, where Chairmen of Provincial clubs who in recent times have reached a Cup Final (St Mirren, Dundee United, Hearts, Queen of the South, etc) always come out and ask the rhetorical question," if only we could get the extra 10,000 who came to the game today to come every week". Well 50 or 60 years ago they might have come, but with virtually no games televised and so few alternative sports and leisure pursuits there was such a demand now the whole town or family will only turn up when there actually is a cup final.

When I was a boy we went to football every week even if our beloved Thistle were away at say Aberdeen or Dundee, my Dad always found another game for us to go to. Likewise we would go to many a big European game at Ibrox or Parkhead as he tried to educate me on the bigger picture of watching classy European teams. For years we would go to cup finals just for the experience and to enjoy the special day. I don't think my Dad was unique as we often bumped into other folk he knew who supported other clubs. Maybe it was just a Glasgow thing; but anyway it has died out. I can remember supporting Aberdeen or Hibs or Dundee in semi -finals at a packed Hampden Park. Changed days when now it is hard enough to get even the most loyal of fans to go to a semi-final.

The strategy for working with Temporary fans: Timing crucial. Link event to social activity. Give reasons to watch other than just to watch the game. Give information about sport and the event.

LOCAL: *Identifies with geographical areas that they were born/grew up in/live in. For example supporting your home town team/following athletes who came from where you live etc.*

In Scottish terms this is a huge struggle as our football is dominated by the Rangers and Celtic. Often people have commented that it is no different to what it is like in Spain or Germany or England. The difficulty we have in Scotland is that with only 5 million folks in the mix there are just not enough fans to go around when you take out the disproportionate amount of fans left for the other clubs. With, England, Spain, Germany and France having huge cities and in many cases distinct cultural differences between the cities or regions that they represent then there is more fans to go around. I have often said to football fans in England in you dropped an average championship side such as say Crystal Palace into the SPL they would be the third biggest club in the league just based on their average gate. This is something we need to accept and try to work around.

Two giant clubs winning everything is hardly an inducement to attracting new fans. "Roll up, roll up- we will never win the league might flirt with relegation and on average reach a cup final every 25 years, Come follow us it will be fun". This seems to dispense with the very basic human desire to try to improve and to win. Few people go into anything in life from a starting position of knowing you will not win. This hits again the point about the lack of competition. In the past rather than face this fact the SPL gave even more revenue to Celtic and Rangers rather than looking at the American system (in all their professional sports) where they try to make it more competitive by having an even distribution of accumulated wealth. If Celtic and Rangers have massive fans bases does it make more sense to give them even more money or is it better to try to make the league more competitive? If it is more competitive their fans will enjoy it more and so will other fans that are more likely to come to watch on a more regular basis.

There is more chance of fighting against this tide the further away you are from Glasgow; but even then the lure of the silverware or the excitement of the big crowds and European football has an impact on the successful recruitment of local fans. Likewise the fact that if you are in Aberdeen you can watch a host of Dons games on the TV means it is harder to get you to pick up the baton for your local club.

The strategy for working with Local fans: Give fans a stake in their local team. Stage community events. Build and maintain local identity.

DEVOTED: *Strong association; tends to be team based. Social factors such as reference group, culture, motivation, learning etc., are key. Typically planned purchase behaviour. For example, a season ticket holder who, when it comes to the weekend that is their sole interest, all other part of life are nullified (family, work etc).*

In a Scottish sense these are the fans we just can't get enough of and unfortunately they are a breed apart. These fans are in decline even at our largest clubs. The problem we have is that football has never modernised, been inventive, or seen itself as a product. Instead for many years we have allowed our game to be controlled by many small minded parochial committee men and suits who patrol the boardrooms of the league bodies and clubs. Great strides have been made since the McLeish report and in particular at the governing bodies level there is a real feeling that change is no longer a dirty word, but an essential word that is on the agenda to help save the game. I really do believe we have some very good people working at the leagues and at the SFA, and my concern is that they can only do so much to lead. What really has to change is the self preservation mentality which has to be replaced by the desire to look at the bigger picture. The time for evolution has come and gone now we need to be thinking about revolution if we want to get growth back into the sport that we love.

The strategy for working with Devoted fans: Give detailed team/player information. Offer branded products and services. Maintain and augment the event experience.

FANATICAL: *Addictive but controlled behaviour. More extreme version of the devoted fan, social factors extremely important. Always planned purchase behaviour. For example, the football fan that attends every game home and away; has wallpaper the same colour as house, car colour the same; naming a child after a player or manager of whom they had much affection for.*

In Scotland we use the term fan to describe anybody who has an affiliation with a club of choice. In this scenario described by our academic we again have seen the demise of this type of supporter. This sector will continue to decline unless clubs start to evolve their marketing strategies to get more of these fans. Little research has been done on how you become one of these fans and of course even less research has been done on how you might attract and retain what is the most important customer in football for both the home and away clubs.

The strategy for working with Fanatical fans: Give ways for fan to demonstrate loyalty and identify with the team or individual. Personalised marketing with events, facilities, products and services only available to 'true' fans.

DYSFUNCTIONAL: *Obsessive, dangerous anti-social behaviour. The team or individual is the ONLY important thing of their lives. Obsessively planned purchased behaviour. For example, a fan who will be obsessed with team or sports athlete to the exclusion of everything else. Borderline religious following.*

Some might put this category into the bin but so many of these individuals if handled properly they could become a useful asset to the clubs. The key is ensuring they have some sort of control over their outputs which is not easy. Many of these Obsessives have become "keyboard warriors" which of course is a very dangerous situation for clubs given the power of social media. It is easy to say "ignore it"; but if you look at the fans power momentum in Scotland over the summer there is an argument that says that this galvanised fans more so much more than what the press did.

　　Strategy for working with Dysfunctional fans: De-marketing important to curb and modify socially unacceptable behaviour. Education programmes. Segregation.

Football insights fan types: Understanding the football fan*
My consultancy which launched in March 2012 is called Football Insights and its purpose is to provide the football clubs with the necessary tools to know and understand customers better. As part of some research that we did for the SFA (that they did not actually use) we drilled a bit deeper and provided a more precise picture of just who the various groups of fans are and what they do and of course most importantly how we can interact with them as customers. This work was based on consultancy conducted for Patrick Thistle FC.

*see loyalty ladder chart in photo section page 16

Closer to home - our Scottish fans
Before we can even think about trying to get more fans into our grounds it is essential that we try to understand our fans and how they fit into each club. There is no definitive version of this fans profiling and for FOOTBALL INSIGHTS research purposes we believe that this is as a complete picture as possible to create. If you think you don't feel you fit into one of these categories then let me know and I will review it in future. If you can imagine a loyalty ladder then the higher up the ladder you go the more important the fan is to the club and how much they can generate as income for the club.

Football diehard: - 24% of fans

Never misses a game home and away unless they can help it. Without doubt the most loyal of all fans. They would not miss a game except in extreme circumstances (serious family illness or bereavement, etc.) or indeed if cost prohibits it. This is sometimes seen with Old Firm fans who can no longer afford the foreign trips that were once the norm. These diehards will always ensure that key decisions such as a weddings or holidays are always taken out with the football season. This is a sector that is diminishing and in our research we have found fewer of these fans than we might have historically expected.

Committed regular: - 28% of fans

A season ticket holder who unlike the *Diehard* does not need to see every game in the flesh. They take in the odd "local" away match. For example if you were a Partick Thistle fan you might go to see them away at Hamilton Accies or Falkirk but a trip to Dundee might be deemed too far and if the clubs were in Europe these fans would be a bit more selective and try to attend wherever possible. The key with this group is to ensure that they don't drop down to become a *Committed Occasional* as this will take the revenue away from being guaranteed to become possible or probable income.

Committed occasional: - 30% of fans

Goes to around half the home games or maybe less; but not enough to merit buying a season ticket at the club he loves. Would like to go to more games; but other commitments such as family and or work or finance, means that this is not possible. Always the fans that football clubs should try to convert to buy a season ticket as they are the most likely to be converted to become a *Committed Regular*.

Historical occasional: - 15% of fans

Always been a fan but only manages to a few games a season. They have dropped down the loyalty ladder and the income they subsequently give to the club has diminished. A very dangerous category to have fans in as they can quite easily fall down completely and become *lapsed lovers*. Most fickle of fans who find it easy to do other things on a Saturday where football is now just part of a repertoire of things they do rather than being the core of their weekend activity.

Walk in: - 1% of fans

Loves football just looking for a game in the area or a place they are visiting. *"So I am in Dumfries and I wonder if the Queens are playing at home today, yip great I'll go along and see them."* Much more prevalent in the halcyon days of the 1950s through to the early 1980s. Now however it is a rare sight and many of the futile marketing campaigns seen across the county are aimed at this market segment when they should be looking at others further up the loyalty ladder. What I found in my time at Stirling Albion was that we quite often got tourists coming in on this category.

Distant lover: - 2% of fans

Fans in exile who don't get to matches as much as they would like. Through time the passion wanes and this sector becomes the hardest to keep on side, tends to erode passion and it becomes harder to engage with them on a day to day basis. They can come a few times a season for big matches but you are limited to what value you can extract from them. The internet has helped as has Social Media, but it is hard to do much in this sector.

International Lover:

Not really worth mentioning in the Scottish context (except that it does link *Distant Lovers* above) unlike the English Premier League who have attracted on a club by club basis. There are massive "new digital fans" abroad but we have only fans of Celtic and Rangers in this category - usually in far flung spots from the days of the Empire in Australia and Canada. The difference to our clubs is that there is virtually no chance to monetise this and it remains to them the mythical golden egg that is just out of reach.

Lapsed lover:

They used to watch the team and can be encouraged out for big occasions - such as cup finals, play offs or unique events (testimonials or celebratory event relating to past glories) but apart from that you will never see them. When they die off the family connections are often lost and history is broken and can't be reclaimed. If had a pound for every person who I met who told me their Grandfather use to be a Thistle fan I would be able to make a sizable contribution to the club's playing budget. This is no urban myth for if you look at the record attendance of 49,838 in the 1920s then there was a lot of grandfathers and great grandfathers to lose.

AWAY FROM HOME - INTERESTED OTHERS AND THE AWAY SUPPORT

Away fans:

These will be in one of the categories above

Armchair fans:

They only watch games on TV. They are most likely to have previously found a place higher up the loyalty ladder; but dropped right off the spectrum probably from getting out the habit of going to matches. Other circumstances such as taking up other sports, having a family or changes at the club or indeed a general dissatisfaction with the game they used to love takes then to the TV screens. From the League's perspective the simple message is that you can't have it both ways and if fans drop of the loyalty ladder you just need to be thankful that they still buy a Sky or ESPN subscription. Of course there is a danger that their loyalty to Scottish Football will decline as they expand horizons through watching the more glamorous Spanish and English leagues and that is a danger for losing revenue for our leagues.

For work:

Those who will attend football matches either for corporate reasons or because they work for the club or other football body.

6 HAVE YOUR SAY FANS REPRESENTATIVES AT ALL CLUBS

Fan involvement the way forward

On the back of driving the campaign to buy Stirling Albion it is maybe no surprise to hear me advocating that ALL clubs should be forced by legislation from the league to have an elected fans' representative on the Board of the club. Since I started writing this book I have now been employed by Supporters Direct Scotland and one of the very important parts of this role is to develop and support fans getting better representation. I should point out that this concept is something that I have been thinking about for a few years now - just in case you think I am using this space to talk about a manifesto pledge!

Wider acknowledgement of the role of fans has come from UEFA which has met with supporter representatives at the House of European Football in Nyon as part of continuing dialogue between European football's governing body and fans – a lifeblood of the game. Earlier this year UEFA was represented at the annual meeting by some really big hitters including President Michel Platini; Peter Gilliéron, chairman of the UEFA Fair Play and Social Responsibility Committee; the CEO of UEFA Events SA, David Taylor; adviser to the UEFA President and of course former CEO of the SFA, William Gaillard; and various members of the UEFA administration.

The supporters groups' delegates came from Football Supporters Europe (FSE), Supporters Direct (SD) Europe, and the Centre for Access to Football in Europe (CAFE). UEFA and the fan groups have now met five times to discuss issues of mutual interest.

The FSE network is an independent, representative and democratically organised grassroots network of football fans with members in 40 countries across Europe.

SD Europe aims to create conditions in which supporters can secure influence and ownership of football clubs, and promotes the value of supporter ownership to sports fans, empowering them to set up supporters' trusts or become members of existing trusts.

Various matters were on the agenda, including official fan groups' relations with UEFA, the European football family and the European political authorities; ticketing and security-related matters; disciplinary matters; supporter liaison work; facilities and access to matches for disabled spectators; supporters and UEFA EURO 2012; how to strengthen the relationship between UEFA and supporter representatives.

The groups gave presentations of their current work and activities, as well as future plans and projects, and put forward proposals to take the relationship forward. UEFA in particular gave an update about its financial fair play measures, which are being put into operation to introduce more discipline into club football finances and bolster European football's stability and well-being.

UEFA pledged to give the supporters' groups as much support as possible in their activities, and thanked them for the work being undertaken on behalf of football fans across Europe as part of overall efforts to improve the game. Encouraging noises were made about the customers.

"UEFA is the home of football, and the fans are part of the football family," Michel Platini told the supporters' delegates in Nyon. "It is important to have you here, and we are certainly here to listen to you – we take your views into consideration when we can. Football belongs to the fans as well, and it's a pleasure to be able to exchange views and hear your ideas." In fact it is even implicit in UEFA's Vision Europe Document which stated that - *in an ideal world all clubs would be controlled and run by their members e.g. supporters - according to democratic principles.*

So can we push that message to get more influence or even ownership - the answer is yes!

Club ownership - who cares and does it matter?

Having helped saved Stirling Albion and run the club for over a year I have moved on to pastures new and left the club to its own devices. The question that still haunts me is that in these turbulent times for football is what is the best model for ownership of Scottish football? In the case of Stirling Albion the fans borrowed money from some of its wealthier fans to buy out a conventional old school owner in the shape of local businessman and long term benefactor Peter McKenzie. The idea being that fans' ownership is the way forward, to ensure democracy and to ensure that the club survived. Of course survival and sustainability are one of the key reasons why fans want to protect their club and to ensure its survival. There are many other Community schemes that can work just as effectively and have had success across Scotland. We should be proud of the fact that Dundee, Clyde and Stenhousemuir take our democratically controlled clubs to four. It is a long way behind the Bundesliga, but it is a start and I predict there will be more to follow as the old rich benefactor model has simply run out of steam and money!

Of course buying any club is just the start of the adventure and the challenge is once you have it you have to grow the business - if you want success. How you manage to do that in a market that is in decline is of course hard to deliver. One of the key learning I hope those left at Stirling take from the experience is that it is critical that you have football knowledge and commercial experience in the Boardroom and that "owners" need to become a different type of fan. So it is possible to do?

As we previously mentioned the clubs we know and love all had their origins in local fan/player ownership and grew into something completely different to that extent. Supporter ownership of football clubs is not something strange, or new, or confined to the margins of European football. Ownership is part of the fabric of the history of our game and it is a living breathing history that continues to be written not just in Europe but in Scotland too.

When we look at who owns clubs we can't ignore the fact that fans are the most important financial stakeholders and that anybody else involved in the club is just passing through. We have already talked about the level of loyalty that fans give. It is not like shopping at Tesco and finding out that Asda is a cheaper option just down the road. Once you stepped in the tradition of your club you are very unlikely to move away from it except when you die! That unique level of loyalty makes football supporters the lifeblood of the game – economically, culturally and socially they are wedded to the club infrastructure through the commitments they make willingly to support their clubs. They invest in them not just with their cash; but just as importantly with the fabric of emotions they bring and the time they invest in them on a long term basis (home and away). It is for many a type of religion. Unfortunately, the last twenty years has seen football car crashes where the false gods have come in and used clubs to enhance their business profile or their ego and have taken the clubs most precious asset with them.

Supporters invest willingly in clubs whether they are successful or not and they support the employment of others. To paraphrase the late great Bill Shankly, "it is not about profit it is about something far more important than that." This lifelong commitment means that these supporters are unique customers and as such their involvement in the governance of football clubs and the game as a whole brings an important added value, namely a long term interest in its sustainability. So how could we ignore them?

Many fans strive for club ownership and in the past year we have seen St Mirren look to a community ownership which seems to have floundered, as the raising of funds for a club with no debt and owners who want to maximise the return in investment is a bridge to far. However, I don't think that story is finished and I do hope it will have a happy ending for the Buddies. At Motherwell a scheme has also been launched by The Well society offering fans to be part of history. After 13 years of a very mixed service, John

Boyle has decided to exit and he has agreed to gift his shares to an independent trust which will be administered by four trustees, who are directors of the Club's board.

Fans will be able to participate in the ownership of the club through the, "The Well Society". To participate there will be a variety of memberships available which involve putting in from just a few pounds to a whopping £25,000 a season which will allow fans to buy shares and elect members of the Well Society to the board of Motherwell F.C. On the one hand it seems to be providing fans with a means of voicing their opinions at board level at a cost and the shares that were being gifted to them seem to have to be bought? Confused? I am too as the documentation clearly says that the club might be sold on if it is in the right interest of "the club".

Of course the other challenge with outright fans ownership is that it is as complete lottery as to who you get in the boardroom. Democracy is great, but bear in mind that the Monster Raving Looney Party and other extremists still attract voters. Supporters' Trusts as I have found out in my particular journey attract a lot of strange and interesting people and that is me being polite about it. More often than not they are - fans - who have very little business experience and of course have no experience of working in the football industry. It is important that we recognise that football is a business first and foremost and that to get the most out of it you need people with the right commercial skills to get involved in it and help will be required to help many groups to facilitate this.

So what about the bigger fish? Well with assets such a stadium worth millions and many with debts that are almost of Greek proportions, there seems to be very little chance of others joining the queue which is a shame as there is a model that could work - the much talked about Bundesliga model. Here in Scotland ironically one of the clubs that has been much maligned for its past indiscretions who probably have it just about right is Livingston where the fans own 50% and businessmen with some financial muscle own the other half. Whether more follow remains to be seen; but from the number of people I have spoken to the consensus is that the status quo is starting to sound like a bad record. In the SPL given that nobody would want to buy Kilmarnock with a debt reported to be around £9million is it not time to get the fans involved in looking at ways they might take the club forward - even if it is starting from scratch.

There is no doubt that there is political will to push football as an industry to actually recognise and appreciate the role it plays in society and with its consumers too. For far too long fans (the customers) have been treated with distain and yet if you were to measure their loyalty it would go off the scale compared to that shown to any other product or service that they might buy. If there was Tesco Club card or Nectar Card for football fans it really would start to show a uniform approach. If you look at all the major sports in the USA you start to get an understanding of how sporting integrity and the strength of the league benefiting the whole league not just the big clubs is the way to go - that is if you want to improve standards and increase competition. Now if fans had their way I am sure that landscape would change.

Fans involvement in ownership of Clubs in Scotland

The table below gives an idea of how fans influence in Scottish football is changing with more power of course comes more responsibility and with senior clubs such as Dundee, Stirling Albion, Clyde and Stenhousemuir having various community ownership models it means that the influence at Hampden Park as well as boardrooms will continue to grow.

	2001	2011
Controlling Stake in Club	0	7
Supporter-Directors on Club Board	2	10
Supporter Shareholding in Club	2	31
Supporters-Trusts	4	34
Members	800	15000

You can see in chapter 19 just exactly what fans at clubs across the country want to happen to our game in the future. Part of our plan thanks to significant funding from the Scottish Government is to help try to help ordinary fans get an organised voice in the game and to make sure that voice is heard loud and clear at Hampden Park.

At this point it might be worth looking at how these principles apply at Barcelona FC:

■ Open memberships to everybody
■ Democratic member control
■ Economic participation from the membership
■ Independence from "the club"
■ Educate members to participate
■ Cooperation with other cooperatives
■ Concern for the community

Now those might sound idealistic but nobody can say that in this instance that it does not work.

for it
- *brings democracy to the game*
- *makes fans responsible for own destiny or gives them a say*
- *enhances the community values*
- *provides a good platform for attracting a bigger audience*
- *allow fans to understand the mechanics of running a professional club*
- *4 senior clubs in Scotland now run with Community Interest model*

against it
- *problems with large clubs either ownership model Celtic being a plc) or Kilmarnock saddled with £9m of debt means it can't be a universal solution*
- *democracies are great but often the people involved do not have the right skill sets*
- *limited access does not guarantee you can do anything as in the example of Dundee where fans owed over 20% of the club and had fans on the board but still went into administration*

WHAT OUR EXPERTS THINK:

Donald McGruther
I think there is no going back on this one now that the fans have started to have their say. It is after all their clubs and the current owners should be seen as just guardians of the club.

Bryan Jackson
I believe in fans involvement in clubs either through ownership and/or representation on the board. However, fans only tend to come forward at a crisis time at a club and that is a real shame as club owners are often missing a huge opportunity not widening the engagement that they could have with ordinary fans. However, more fans' trusts are beginning to obtain majority ownership of clubs, sometimes as a necessity, and it will be interesting to see if these developments become positive and encourage others to follow suit.

Jocky Scott

I guess the existing boards would all say that they are fans too so I am not sure where that leads you. I guess it all depends on the people. When I worked with you (the author) and Steven Leiper at Stirling it was fine; but after you left they didn't have a clue.

John Blackley

I think fans having some sort of say is essential and I am pleased that clubs are at last wakening up to this fact. Running a club though should be the preserve of people who know the industry not fans.

Steven Tweed

Football clubs are a business, fans are coming to fore just now, rightly or wrongly, the reason this is happening is because clubs are doing so poorly. They are in there, lifting these clubs up, you have to find a balance between fan involvement at boardroom level and how the club is run. If someone has put a lot of money in to a football club then it should be them who has the final say in how the club is run.

Davie Hay

More than ever football needs its fans and I think that it is important that the game evolves to recognise that more and allows them a voice at club level and also at Hampden Park.

Kevin McGoldrick

I work at a fan owned club and it doesn't feel any different except that there are more people involved and from a football perspective as long as they let the professionals do that then I think it works.

Alex Smith

I think that fans do need a role but is it essential that what they should be doing is considered. Of course it all comes down to who the people are. You know I have had a disappointing experience at Stirling Albion since you guys (Goodwin and Leiper) left and I guess it all comes down to the quality of the people involved whether they be fans or ordinary directors.

Des McKeown

I am against it. You can look at it from a fan's perspective but you also have to look at it from a chairmen or a manager's perspective. I think fans can definitely play a part but I think some clubs have a fans representative on there because he is voted on by the supporters club effectively. I had one at Stenhouesmuir and he wasn't the best. There are some football clubs where fans think they can run their football club better than the board. I think football clubs should be run by people that do not have just an emotional connection – they need to be able to offer something to the club.

Ebbsfleet down in England have been a bit of a freak show for me. I think it is interesting and quirky, but I wouldn't want other clubs run like that. I know the Coventry chairman during the earlier part of this season was floating an idea, that if the fans in the ground could text in the ground who they would want substituted he was wanting to make revenue off the text cost! It was just ridiculous. Ridiculous! It was blown out the water anyway; but in terms of the partnership element...I know you have got this down later on – club partnership. No, sorry... I'll have a look at that. A community partnership I think football clubs should, certain football clubs, in fact most football clubs should be a community sporting hub. I think that could facilitate more people to get involved in lots of different ways. In terms of football decision making, I think that should be left to people who are voted on to that board, to make those decisions.

David Mackinnon

Fans must be represented by a presence in the Boardrooms at clubs throughout the country.

This must though be controlled by an independent CEO as fans in Boardrooms, including some current Club Chairman and Directors, sometimes make decisions with their hearts rather than their heads and this often leads to irrational decisions being made.

When I was appointed as CEO of Dundee there was a Board consisting of eight fans. Eight superbly dedicated people led by two great Dundee men, Peter and Jimmy Marr, guys with the club very firmly in their hearts.

When I presented my business plan which included a clear-out of players receiving top end SPL wages in their second SPL season, there was dismay that some of the board member's favourite players were included in the list. Eventually I was able to convince them of the reality that administration would be on the horizon if we didn't address the huge wage percentage. They reluctantly agreed to the plan but I suspect many in the boardroom resented having to lose some players who had become mini legends.

The statement that fans are the life blood of a club has never been more appropriate and without their presence in the decision making process then situations like the tragedy at Rangers will no doubt happen again.

Jamie McGowan

I think as we have already seen this season fans have an important part to play in football politics. It is really important that fans have a voice.

Jackie McNamara

I think there is no going back since the Rangers crisis. Football has to listen to the fans and I think it is only right that those who pay our wages have a say in their club.

Darren Jackson

I think having fans having some sort of representation is good; but when you are talking about fans you need to be careful in terms of how many you invite into the decision making process. What works for me is that it gives the fans the input and a bit of shared responsibility and understanding of how the big picture in football works.

Sandy Clark

I can't see this going away as an issue as the fans have started to get a voice and I think over the years many of our smaller clubs will go back into the community and do what Clyde, Stirling etc have done and why not? Obviously as that happens it means that the fans will get a bigger voice at the SFA which they have never had before. I think it is good news but I am not sure it will work at the bigger clubs where control and power remains key to the boardroom.

CONCLUSION

Fans might not own all the shares of a club; but they are the heart and soul of the club and are its biggest asset. There is a need for them to have a bigger say in how the clubs they love are run. RATHER, as in many cases, than waiting on a crisis to call for support for the fans, there should be a process of getting fans involved on a more formal basis. Our work at Supporters Direct Scotland will be in a position to further facilitate this and we would encourage all fans and clubs to work with us.

7 CREATIVE WAYS TO SAVE SCOTTISH FOOTBALL!!!! – BREAKING THE RULES

Before my business, Football Insights, got into full swing I spent some time doing marketing work for Stirling Albion and for Partick Thistle, the team I support. We looked at some detailed market research to get an understanding of what fans really wanted. Of course with any type of survey the key to finding out real insights is to ask the right type of questions. The vast majority of football clubs have in my experience either paid little attention to what fans - their customers- really feel or have never deviated from the obvious question sets. Before we started the Football Insights business we asked 10 clubs when they last asked for their fans' views. From the 10 clubs we asked the average length of time that had elapsed was around seven years. Can you imagine any other business in the world that would ignore the views of their most valuable customers for such a long period of time? I firmly believe that there are several reasons why this has happened.

No marketing expertise at Boardroom level means no proper joined up marketing strategies

a) There is just not the marketing expertise in Scottish Football to help drive the business strategy.

In other businesses there is a marketing department that helps drive growth and hone the business strategy. There are undoubtedly some good people working very hard in Scottish football but there are very few clubs with a real marketing presence at board level to drive the business forward. As a result the clubs and associations are stale and not alive to pushing the boundaries and implementing new methods in their approach to dealing with their customers. It might just reignite the game that we all love.

We continue to ignore our most valuable asset - our loyal fans

b) If you ask questions that you don't want to hear the answers to- it can be a bit of a problem for you.

A perfect example of this was the Supporters Direct Survey which had a huge response of over 4000 fans. Over 86% of fans wanted a top league of at least 16 teams. Yet the SPL felt at that time that it was their remit to ignore what the fans wanted. Of course it is understandable as they faced a potential income loss of up to £20 million in lost revenue from TV deals. Frustratingly for the fans, no detailed explanation of this substantial figure has ever been made clear to the supporters. A similar figure was mentioned if Rangers were not kept in the top flight. We seem to be surviving without this big £20 million - probably because the deals were renegotiated successfully which is what would happen if the league structure changed. It is a pretty basic economic argument that if you only had two potentially exciting events rather than four, then the value and the desire to see them would increase dramatically and so what you could charge at the gate. Would Wimbledon or the F1 Grand Prix sellout if there were four of them a year - of course not.

Given how much misinformation and cries of Armageddon that has been circulating over the years, it is a really big ask of fans to accept it and to move on. There also has not been any dialogue on how the fans issues might be addressed or serious consideration as to how the two opposite views might be brought closer together for the good of Scottish football. To the fans it looks like propaganda and there is no trust between the supporters and the controlling bodies of football in this country.

Fans at games is the most important thing

c) Real live fans are of secondary importance to the SPL and the clubs.

TV has been allowed to drive our football strategy - meaning armchair fans are deemed to be more important than real fans. This means our game is off kilter and the balance needs looked at. We need brave leadership to achieve this as well as having the desire to make sure league earnings are distributed fairly.

As highlighted above, the fans that turn up week in week out season after season are of secondary importance to the SPL and the clubs they represent. Unlike Sky and ESPN they are not allowed to sit down and discuss the revenue that they might bring in the industry each year. The TV audience is what is driving the game and aside of having games at inconvenient times to suit the sofa audiences, more power is now vested in the offices at ESPN & Sky than those at Hampden. Of course this is very sad and we can only imagine what the late Jim Farry might have thought about this. In his tenure at the SFA he fought long and hard to protect Scottish Football from what he felt was the constant intrusion into our game. Often viewed as backward looking and insular, we can in retrospect look back over his many outbursts against "too much TV" as being almost clairvoyant. As for the £20 million that would be lost to the game, maybe we should take the opportunity to shut down, reboot and start again with clubs paying what they can afford to pay and we all collectively work to get families into our grounds rather than sit back and accept that the sofa brigade cannot be allowed to dictate the future of the game we love. If we accepted the loss and had the necessary adjustment in what our objectives were, then I believe the whole country would benefit from paying players what they are worth. It would also lead to every club nurturing their own talent and a far stronger national team emerging as a consequence of this.

Outside of football as I write this book there has been an outcry about the salary paid to Ian Craig, the MD of Edinburgh bus operator, Lothian Buses.. Questions were raised right up to Holyrood about Mr Craig's substantial £208,137 salary for running the majority of the Capital's buses.However there was no huge outcry and nobody seemed to bat an eyelid at what was going on at Rangers. Martin Bain was getting a reported figure in excess of £600,000 a year - more than the Prime Minister and First Minister each earn. The PM has to make do with just £142,000 for running the UK and the Coalition and the FM gets £135,605 for running a county of over 5 million people rather than an unprofitable football club of 300 employees. How many season tickets had to be sold just to pay him?

So the issue is that Scottish football needs to be brave enough to ask the customers what they think. Of course in doing so if you ask them the same old questions, there should be little surprise that you will get the same old answers! The real issue that we have had in Scottish football is that it has been the same old story without any real movement in making actual changes. There is no business in the world that can afford to ignore its loyal customers or, even worse, make their valued customers feel frowned upon or that their views don't matter.

As a leading American online entrepreneur Charles Schwab commented, "At the end of every day, having a clientele that speaks well of you, that's the largest source of business. I don't care what kind of business you're in. Clients referring us to their friends or relatives is so much more powerful than any advertising we could ever do." As the league don't advertise (they don't need to as they have free press coverage) then they should be utilising this marketing gift to much greater effect.

As the legendary Jock Stein said:

"Without fans who pay at the turnstile, football is nothing. Sometimes we are inclined to forget that. You could have the greatest game in the world but without fans it is meaningless."

How right he was and 40 years later the football industry is still in denial. You just need to look at what Jamie Oliver did with his campaign to get decent school dinners for kids across the UK or what Hugh Fernley Whittingstall did to help eradicate intensive chicken farming and his big fish fight to get a change in policy from the supermarkets to offer sustainable products. It did take a huge effort but eventually even the mighty Tesco could not ignore public opinion.

If our clubs and the SPL want a game that is broadcast around the globe with empty stadiums then they should continue to ignore the fans who have been voting with their feet for years and will just give in and avoid the cold, rain and expensive season ticket prices and stay at home and join the sofa brigade. If we fast forward 30 years maybe the future of the game will just see closed doors games all played at Ravenscraig or Toryglen and televised to the shrinking audience who have found futuristic versions for Total Wipeout and the X Factor more compelling. Bleak, scary, unrealistic but who knows. What we can be sure of is that fundamental change is needed or we face a very uncertain and potentially hazardous future. What we can of course say is that unless some radical plans are formulated and fast then the landscape will change and it will not be a positive change.

Football of course is different; it has always been different and always will be different. This is how many in the game see it through the rose tinted spectacles adorning their noses. I beg to differ and believe that if we just changed one word in football it could have a major impact in the future of the game. If the word FAN was eliminated from the dictionary used by clubs and league authorities and the word CUSTOMER inserted in its place then football might just have a chance of surviving. If we grasp the opportunity these loyal, dedicated customers afford us and we work with them to give them more rather than dismiss them then the game might just prosper.

What I wanted to achieve with the research for both Partick Thistle and Stirling Albion was to try to extract as much data that had statistical significance as possible, as well as testing some innovations to see if we could get the fans to buy in. At larger clubs the data would have formed the basis of helping drive a strategy that would be used in conjunction with their CRM (customer relationship marketing) but, for these wee community clubs, it was just a matter of knowing your audience then the better you would know your fans. I was astonished that both of these clubs knew so little about their fans and that in the past there really was no long term strategy in place to deliver against a set of objectives. As a result of conducting the work both clubs are in a far better place after the work than before it and have a much better understanding of their customers. Of course this work also allowed me to ask some interesting questions too and with interesting questions there will be more interesting answers.

The concepts

These are what they say they are - just concepts - and will need more work to get them past the developmental stage. Some of the concepts such as summer football and league reconstruction have been talked about before but others hopefully offer something fresh. The purpose of this book is to try to look at these existing concepts as well as developing some new concepts that I hope will stimulate some debate at a time when Scottish Football is probably at its lowest ebb in its 130 year history. Whilst the McLeish report did a great job on governance it didn't address or offer solutions regarding the stale, expensive product served up every Saturday at a ground near you. As I said, like all concepts, these need consideration and the added value of many other opinions to further develop them into rounded workable solutions. Doing nothing is no longer acceptable. So I just hope that somebody picks up that mantle and soon!

8 LET'S CHANGE WHEN WE PLAY FOOTBALL - THE 3PM WATERSHED

Like most football fans I am something of a traditionalist. There is just something special about looking forward to going to see your team play at 3 o'clock on a Saturday afternoon. It is a tradition that is enjoyed up and down the country by football fans of all clubs; but it has not always been that way. In the distant past before the introduction of floodlights in the 1950s games did not always get played at 3 o'clock in the winter as it was just too dark to get them finished before the winter gloom set in. Of course now the might of TV has meant that it is the programme schedulers at SKY who decide when games kick off.

As we all know the loyalty of fans has been used as a tool to manipulate the once sacred fixture lists to ensure that the armchair fans are fed a diet of continuous football from every league in the world. How I remember some of my bachelor days some 12 years back when myself and my flatmate and massive Hibs fan Alan Ramsay tried to see how many games we could watch on TV in one weekend. I think our record was around nine before we had some sort of football overload! Different countries have their own traditions, or needs, dictated by climate, or working patterns which dictate when games are played. I always feel that it is a touch surreal, in fact just plain weird, to go to a game at 8pm on a Sunday when I am in Spain on holiday. Of course no matter what country you live in the broadcasters have now ensured that there always is a constant stream of live football from La Liga down to the Football Conference. As punters, the diet of football that is given to us is virtually on tap whether you want it or not. The business of football needs to recognise this and respond accordingly. I tried a little bit of research by asking 120 fans who no longer had satellite TV a question:"Now that you no longer have satellite football on TV are you more likely to go and watch live football?" 76% said "yes", 17% said "maybe" and 7% said "no". Of course with a sedentary audience on the super football highway the chances of even the very best marketing brains creating something compelling that would pull you from the Barclays' Premier League or Barcelona and Real Madrid's La Liga's performances to see Ayr United v Stenhousemuir is unlikely.

Of course globalisation is a huge part of the shift in the power of TV and that has had, certainly in England, just about killed off the poor old traditionalists. It was interesting to note that since the start of 2012, Manchester United played 18 football matches home and away. Of these, just one has kicked off at 3pm on a Saturday. Just 20 years ago, anything other than a 3pm Saturday kick-off was still the exception and fans just took it for granted. TV took that pleasure away. Now, thanks to television, the top teams suffer more than most and it seems that they rarely appear at the old appointed Saturday hour. In season 2011/12, the two FA Cup semi-finals were played at 12.30pm on Saturday and 6pm on Sunday while the Cup Final, whose 3pm Saturday kick-off time was once a national institution was moved to after 5.00pm. Why does it happen? Well it's obviously because of TV schedules. The FA were happy to admit that. "The later time maximises a bigger domestic and global TV audience for broadcasters". It is not the first time that profits have been put in front of the needs and desires of the fans and it will not be the last. As ever, football puts profit before people. Should real fans just accept this fate or should they try to do something about it? Certainly in Scotland, which is something of a backwater for the colossal digital deals on offer to the English leagues, we have even less of a voice.

Thank Friday it's footie time- let's be different to attract a new audience

I looked at this issue when I was at Stirling Albion and I asked David Longmuir CEO of the Scottish Football League not long after we took over if we could look to play our games on Friday nights. He had no objection to it but he did query how difficult it would be to achieve. The immediate concern was the need to get full league approval, the approval of any particular opponent and, at a local level, trying to get the police to agree given the potential of late-night weekend drinking would mean that they would be stretched to be in attendance.

I wanted to test the viability of the concept as I was somebody who was old enough to remember Tranmere Rovers in the 1970s and early 1980s playing all their home matches on a Friday night to avoid competing against the Merseyside giants of Liverpool and Everton. It must have worked as the "experiment" lasted for years. I guess it was in a time when there were fans who followed more than one team and with so little football on TV and admission prices being low there were many fans who liked to see as many games as they could. Those games are long gone but I was delighted to see that Friday football did get a chance in Scotland with three games which all showed increased attendances. My quest to have a game on a Friday evening was based on my desire just to change the dynamic to see if I could make a fixture more attractive by attracting a different audience. Of course you always run the risk of losing fans who are engrained in the habit. I recall listening at a Patrick Thistle shareholders meeting a few weeks after the Friday game against Morton had been announced and a season ticket holder complained that he was missing the game as it did not suit him and that he was not going to renew his ticket next season because of this. Fans, who needs them? Well as we have been haemorrhaging fans we need to try to do things differently and really work at getting fans into our grounds on a more regular basis.

So Friday football is a good concept and with the selection of the correct fixtures I hope it will continue. It is not however, the complete answer, more a great opportunity and part of a tool box of concepts that can help make the game more attractive and hopefully help attract a new audience.

The one o'clock salute

The first piece of research that we conducted under the Football Insights banner was for Stirling Albion and Partick Thistle. We completed large omnibus surveys. Between both clubs we got just under 3000 responses which was a particular high percentage of fans of both clubs. Like any research the key is in asking the right questions to extract the right insights for the topic you want to explore. In both these surveys I asked the question: "*If it helped your club save money would you agree to play your fixtures at 1pm?*" Over 97% of those fans who completed the survey were happy to agree to drop the 3pm watershed and play at 1pm for the sake of their club. Of course we didn't ask what would fans prefer 1pm or 3pm nor did we ask fans who can't or have little interest in attending at 3pm if this move would help them. If we knew that was a positive then bingo we really would be on to something.

In my own experience, before I had a family, the 3pm kick off was just fine but since the family came along and they are at the ages where they do sports and entertainment "things" it just seems like you have difficulty fitting in things before the 3pm game. So maybe the 1pm is a better time for families? Of course what it does not address is the core issue of WHY there is a continual decline in the traditional football audience. We all know that a constant diet of TV football as well as the vast amount of alternative pursuits that are often less expensive have combined to drive down attendances. The 1 o'clock kick off in some people's eyes might be seen as being radical and I don't think it will change attendances in itself; but for many clubs the cost savings across a season could justify it. Having discussed the costs with several clubs and extrapolated across all the senior clubs in Scotland the savings could be as much as £600,000 which is the equivalent to some of the biggest sponsorships in the Scottish game.

For it

- *Changes the dynamic of the stale set up we have that does not take us forward (same old, same old). Given that we can't stand still and if you are not going forwards you are going backwards, it is worth trying.*
- *It offers a chance to encourage new fans to come to try football*
- *It could work to attract families with this different time slot*
- *It could produce significant floodlighting cost benefits estimated in excess of £600,000 across all of Scottish football*
- *It would help clubs reduce carbon footprint which is something that could be sponsored by an energy company bringing in further additional revenue for clubs*
- *If winter football continues it will mean fans can travel home from away matches for a few hours of daylight rather than after 5pm which could encourage more visiting fans*
- *It could give the lower league clubs a window to attract floating fans of other clubs if it was adopted in the SFL but not the SPL for example*

Against it

- *It will not be liked by traditionalist fans who have a fear of change and who like things just the way they are*
- *Might be difficult to work with hospitality timings where lunch would need to almost be replaced by a brunch*

<u>WHAT OUR EXPERTS THINK:</u>

Donald McGruther

I think anything that starts to challenge the existing state of the game is very much worth considering. We need to get more people into our grounds and to make our football more entertaining. You just need to look at what they do in the USA sports areas to see exactly how they do it. Of course it would be a lot easier if we had better facilities and a better product; but football just does not try hard enough to attract a new audience. Maybe this is something to look at it. Even although I am a traditionalist I still feel that we need to look to a new audience and maybe if this was a package of innovations it would help even show the wider public that football is changing and wants to be a more attractive proposition.

Bryan Jackson

Leaving all the football arguments aside, why not. If it can prove to save clubs money then that could be a great starting point in improving the finances of clubs. I would like to see the whole industry start to shake itself and come up with a plan. I know the McLeish Report was the start of that but I'd like to see more analysis of the financial fundamentals of what has been going wrong in football. The industry, and let's not forget it is an industry, has a terrible track record in the basics of business. Let's be honest about it, spending more money than you have is what causes you problems. Whilst I appreciate there are a number of football and marketing issues on this matter, I like the idea that you start the rebuilding process of clubs collectively saving money. I fear that unless football starts to be more radical in its outlook to its customer then it faces a continual slow decline.

Jocky Scott

I think the biggest problem we face is that parents have got to get their young kids ready for their own football leagues on a Saturday morning. They obviously have to be taken there and taken back. Does that give them enough time at the end of that to take them to a game which kicks-off earlier? Especially if it is an away game where you maybe have to travel an hour to the game. If earlier kick-offs came in to effect then you may reach a stage where parents would have to make a decision, one or the other so to speak. 5pm kick-offs on a full-time basis are probably unrealistic. It would start to cut in to the social life of fans. So you know, I think it is a case of finding out if there is a demand from the fans. How many are turning up for starters, regardless of what time it is? But 3pm on a Saturday is traditionally when football was played and I know we are going to have to change with the times but you know I think regardless of what time you look to play that you are going to have obstacles in some form.

Television plays a massive role in kick-off times nowadays and I think we have all grown to accept it is here to stay. You notice in particular when the Old Firm sides are playing away from home, their schedule is dictated by TV. I notice that in particular these televised SPL away games are failing to get the crowds in like they used to and that isn't dependant on the kick-off time, it can be Saturday, Sunday or midweek.

John Blackley

I am a three o'clock man; without doubt that is the way it always has been and it is the way I always enjoyed it. But crowds are nothing like they were in my day and other traditions have gone by the wayside whether it is two points for a win or not being allowed to pass the ball back to the keeper. The game evolves probably too slowly for its own sake so if it meant that in changing the kick off times I am sure it would be a positive if it saved the club money and brought new people in to watch the game. There is no point in sticking with a tradition like this if there is a better alternative for the good of the game. We professionals could cope with it by altering the pre match routine and it's not as if we have not tried it as matches kick off at bizarre times now due to TV.

Steven Tweed

I think one thing which could be a concern with widespread earlier kick-offs is the drink drive element. If you have been out on the Friday night when do you get in the car to drive from Edinburgh to Dundee or Aberdeen?

I think from a players point of view their pre-match habits would be altered. I used to eat my main meal six hours before a game and that would be difficult for a lot of players to do with earlier kick-offs. I was advised to have my carbohydrate burst well in advance of the game and I would just have something quick like a banana or toast before I went out on the field.

One thing I experienced when I played abroad is that we would always train at the time of our kick-off the week prior. A lot of players used to sleep from 12-2 before the games as well.

Davie Hay

I don't believe the time of the game is the most important aspect, if you do not have a product that people want to see then kick-off times become irrelevant. I can see the argument that changing the kick-off times may lead to a rise in attendances. Scottish football at the moment is a hard sell but I think everyone is willing to look at ideas on how it can improve. I've heard Rod Petrie in recent months speak about how Scottish football needs to get back to 3pm kick-offs, I think that sounds great in theory but I think we have to accept television dictates kick-off times at the top-level, maybe not so much in the lower leagues but I still believe that the quality of football is key in all of this.

Kevin McGoldrick

Looking at early kick-offs from a players and coaching perspective, I think that at the top level obviously you can stay in hotels overnight but when you are part time and travelling and it's away up to somewhere like Peterhead or down to Annan for a 1pm kick off then getting a time to leave becomes very difficult. If you have to get up at the crack of dawn to get there, your preparation is obviously not ideal. Now at the top level you are starting to see more and more games kick-off at 1pm or even earlier and part of the reason is probably because they can stay overnight. But at the lower level I don't think bringing games forward would work very well. However, if it increased crowds and brought more money into the game then it would get approval.

Alex Smith

I think it could work if maybe part of a complete package of reforms. If we had bigger leagues that are less negative, with local talent playing in them during the summer then that would be the ideal situation. I would not worry too much about the actual playing time for us managers and coaches, we just get on with preparing our squads no matter the kick off time. I do like the tradition of a three in the afternoon; but I also like big, excited crowds loving their football and I don't see much of that. Yes by all means change if it is better for fans and can attract more fans in then we should do it. We didn't need much debate when it game to changing kick off times, and days for that matter, for TV.

Des McKeown

I think from a player's perspective earlier kick-off times are not ideal. I think from a football point of view you have had your breakfast then sometimes you go for a pre-match meal, some of the guys aren't totally ready to eat. I have my breakfast a couple of hours before I run a marathon and that sustains me through the race, so I think it would actually suit from a nutritional point of view to eat earlier.

From a playing perspective when I was part-time, I preferred to play at night. I preferred to play at mid-week because my whole diary, my training was at night. But I don't know if that would be the same for full-time players.

Jamie McGowan

Football sold out a long time ago to TV so changing this tradition would not be a problem. Whilst I would not like it myself, if it saves clubs revenue and it brings in a more family audience then let's give it a try. Why not do it across the whole programme one Saturday and market it to the new audience a bit like we did with Friday night football and look at the results. I think football (the SFA & leagues) needs to wake up to the fact there are lots of other family entertainments they are competing against and they just don't try very hard to win new audiences. So let's try it.

Jackie McNamara

I think when I was a player it was difficult to adjust to playing certain games at 3pm, then having Old Firm games played at 12pm. As a player I didn't like it. I found it really hard because my normal pre-match meal would have been pasta or some kind of spaghetti in the hotel. In the morning I found it really hard to eat that kind of stuff. I would end up having Weetabix or something which wasn't right; but I physically couldn't eat pasta in the morning.

The majority of European games or international games I played in were at night. Evenings weren't a problem for me, I would just adjust my times and have a sleep in the afternoon. It was really just the early games that I found difficult to prepare for. Having said that if it worked for the majority and helped me with budgets at Thistle I would adapt pretty quickly.

Darren Jackson

I know from a player's perspective it means a routine change which could be disruptive; but on the positive side I do feel that it could mean that games finish earlier and that it could mean they have more leisure time for their families on a Saturday too. So it might not be a bad thing in particular for the part time players in the lower league. I am thinking in particular where there is long travel involved. Of course the other side of the coin is that you would need to leave earlier to get to the away games. I guess I am sitting on the fence with this one - I can see the benefits but need convinced it is the right thing to do but having said that if it brought more people into watch football, that helps the clubs and creates a better atmosphere, then let's give it a go.

Sandy Clark

I think the hardest thing to change is the fact that the 3pm kick-off is habitual to many supporters, has been that way for a long time. We are creatures of habit; I think it mostly comes down to it being a social thing. The average man or woman is working Monday to Friday and then Saturday has always been a football day. At one point it was the only sport on a Saturday and I don't think there is anything wrong with looking to change but from the supporters' point of view, they are under pressure from external commitments as well. Many fans will already have a routine in place with their family or loved ones. A Saturday afternoon is tribal in many ways; fans go to the match, then go to the pub, have a couple of pints and go up the road. These things are long standing traditions and part of the match day experience. I think it is worth looking at making change if the fans feel that it is necessary. I think in this financial climate if fans are made aware that their club could save money by moving the kick-off forward then they would seriously consider it. Nothing in football is sacred any more, even the FA Cup Final has been devalued with the game becoming earlier each season and the decision to move it to a 5:15 pm kick-off was poor.

David Mackinnon

In any call for change you have to consider if it's change for change sake or will any change be for the better and suit the requirements of today's supporters. The answer would be somewhat irrelevant if the game changed to a summer season; but assuming the season remained as it currently is then anything which has a monetary and environmental benefit must be considered. One caveat would be the logistical side of getting visiting teams and supporters to a game over distance with an early journey start but that would be offset against an early return in relative daylight. Of course geographical restructuring would sort that in the lower leagues!

CONCLUSION

I thought that the professionals would have more resistance to the idea but they correctly identified that TV has changed the goalposts forever and that the 3pm kick off is no longer sacrosanct anyway.

The key with this concept is that more research would need to be done to demonstrate the cost savings and to establish whether it would encourage more fans to come to the games. It is not a difficult piece of research to do and I believe that it is a concept that could indeed be easy to implement and might just lead to more income for clubs. So I would recommend that the football authorities look at conducting that research and if it is positive then it can easily be implemented at a start of a season.

9 SUMMER FOOTBALL
- LET'S MAKE IT HAPPEN

Not surprisingly the topic of summer football seems to come to the fore when the storms of winter appear. There are three obvious issues here: The first is that wind, snow and ice all cause hazards and make the playing of football difficult and often impossible; The second issue and with declining attendances I would argue that the customers (fans) in our research hate having to sit in virtually empty stadiums in the freezing cold, watching a spectacle that is often a fight against the elements as much as it is against the opposition. The third is that it is costing clubs money at the gate, through postponements or indeed the massive cost of turning on the undersoil heating for three days. Dare we even mention the impact that has on the environment which going forward will not be able to be ignored.

In season 2011/12 it was arguably the best weather conditions for several years but we must not forget the two seasons prior which caused mayhem and massive haemorrhaging of money from clubs through cancelled and rearranged fixtures. This is money that the clubs can never get back. Research has shown that rescheduled midweek attendances, in particular for our smaller community clubs, can be around 40% lower than on Saturdays. Nobody has ever asked why this should be; but anecdotally those who live outside the normal catchment area might have difficulty with travel arrangements, certainly with public transport. Younger kids are lost because of school nights and of course it is colder and dark at nights which make the lure of the floodlights a little less appealing. At Stirling we had to launch a Fan Aid campaign as we didn't have a league game from the middle of November until the last week in February. With players still to be paid and other unavoidable costs such as VAT and National Insurance still due, the weather can be more than an imposition. The other problem is that with so few indoor facilities finding suitable training facilities is not ideal and is of course another expense clubs have to incur. Our campaign attracted attention around the globe as the players agreed to play for nothing to allow the club to get back on its feet. I liked the fact that players and fans worked together and we had a lot to thank Manager Jocky Scott and Club Captain Ross Forsyth for helping us make it happen.

Just this year I attended a first division game which had a much lower crowd than the club had anticipated and as I sat next to two club directors who would have looked at home in Siberia (given how many layers they had on). They said to each other, "this is mad who in their right mind would sit out in the freezing cold to watch this dross". I will spare their blushes by not saying what game it was; but the reality is that the mad people who are forced to sit out in these conditions are the ordinary fans who pay for the privilege. Given that fans are now disappearing faster than snow on a winter dyke, then it makes perfect sense that we don't just pay this subject lip service but we actually look to explore how we can integrate a summer league into the schedule for our clubs competing in Europe. Of course there are many who would argue that we are out of Europe so quickly that when we play in these competitions makes little or no difference to when our leagues should start and finish. With a record low European coefficient, the national team struggling along at 56th in the world rankings, crowds at an all-time low, a general worldwide financial meltdown and the only alternative strategy to keep the same or tinker with the existing model.

Can we justify not changing? I don't think we can and if we just step back and look at this problem then there is a very real opportunity for all the clubs. Given the dearth of games in the summer I am sure that this will give the Scottish Leagues a lift and a little competitive advantage.

We know we can get freaky weather in Scotland. As I write this section it is the end of March and this particular week the whole of Scotland is basking in temperatures that are higher than those in Greece or Spain. However you don't need a degree in geophysics to come to the conclusion that our worst weather months are usually between December and February. So avoiding these dark, damp, cold winter months might not totally mean that you can have a postponement free season but it sure as hell gives you a fighting chance. When I was at Stirling Albion, then a first division club, we worked out that we lost around £10,000 - £12,000 a match when a postponed fixture was replayed in midweek. This was between reduced crowds and loss of hospitality revenue and other corporate sales. If you look at bigger clubs like Falkirk or Partick Thistle, the figure might be double that. No business can afford to just accept the loss of revenue without trying to do something about it. No business, apart from football, seems content to grin and bear it. There are defence barriers for the frost and snow such as undersoil heating which is rather expensive and out the reach of most SFL clubs. We have of course seen several instances over the years where in the clubs have not switched the undersoil heating on in time. A few years back Partick Thistle had to postpone a Saturday Scottish Cup tie against Dunfermline because nobody switched the heating system on. It turned out to be an expensive mistake with a rescheduled midweek game meaning 1500 fewer fans. There have been other occasions where clubs have had the undersoil heating system on but the police have refused to allow the game to proceed as the areas surrounding the ground have been deemed too hazardous for spectators.

So how would our new summer league run?- How might it work in practice?

For the sake of argument I have decided for this exercise to keep the league format at 12, 10, 10, and 10 which of course will in the fullness of time change with the potential of league restructuring.

So with 36 games and a summer to play with we can have a mixture of Saturday and midweek games. These would all be scheduled to maximise the earning potential of each participating club in the league.

Our leagues would start at the beginning of March and run until the end of November, with the potential to extend this to the end of December to accommodate cup ties if needed. This would give flexibility to incorporate all the international fixtures required for Euro Championship and World Cup Qualifiers. A decision could be made as and when we start qualifying for the final of these tournaments. That, as they say, would be a problem well worth having but as we have not made it since 1998 I don't think we need to stop this innovation just in case.

For it

When you look at the number of positives associated with changing it beggars belief that we have been tinkering with this broken product for 40 or 50 years without grasping the thistle. I think the few disadvantages that we have in this concept pale into insignificance compared to the performance enhancing possibilities, the marketing opportunities to attract a new audience and the potential for new revenue. I do believe that to get maximum value from this change it would be implemented with a change to the structure of the leagues to take away the predictable four times a season monotony that exists in the current 12 team league structure that is hated by the fans.

So what are we waiting for? Dump the thermals, the hats and gloves and look out the shorts, t-shirts and sunglasses and look forward to helping ourselves to a pre-match barbecue.

- *It changes the dynamic of the stale set up we have*
- *It offers a change to encourage new fans*
- *It could work to attract families*
- *Benefits include selling more summer focussed merchandise*
- *Would help clubs market to a different (family) audience. Two scenarios a) come*

Competing against the big two is hard enough, so why give them a bigger percentage of the pot?

Clydebank were sold down the river by a succession of owners only, to re-emerge as a proud fans-owned junior club.

At Cup Finals everybody and their granny goes; but nobody is able to get them to come back week in week out.

No atmosphere on a cold winters night, we are all sure it would be improved with summer football.

Flowers signalling the death of Gretna as we knew it - is this the end of the benefactor owner model?

The author with the Right Honourable Henry McLeish former First Minister of Scotland at the aunch of the fans parliament - www.scottishfans.org

Kids go free at every ground that would build the fans base and start to create a bit of excitement at grounds.

It is essential that we attract a new audience to football. We don't do enough to attract women and families to games. However, we are less likely to get new fans turning up in the depths of winter.

The rules of building your fanbase:
1. Get customers in
2. Get them to spend once they come in
3. Build your brand (offers) to ensure they come back.

Our Stadiums have changed but the product on the park has not improved.

Empty seats we all have them, so why is it not a priority to try and fill them with attractive offers to new audiences?

Football has free media coverage,
yet doesn't maximise this by using
it to sell marketing campaigns.

Scotland - our glory days are far behind us and yet we seem incapable of any radical changes that would improve our game.

THE SCOTTISH FANS LOYALTY LADDER

(Based on research conducted for Partick Thistle 06/07 season)

'I never miss a game'	**Football Diehard – 24%***	Highest platform - biggest sales target
'I recommend my club and buy a season ticket'	**Committed Regular – 28%**	Satified customer and key sales target
'My circumstances mean I don't go as often as I used to'	**Committed Occasional – 30%**	Half way customer, a key target audience - in danger of going down
'I don't go as often as I used to'	**Historial Occasional – 15%**	Falling down the ladder - hard to convert up - so hold or down
'I used to go every now and then, now I watch it on TV'	**Walk In – 1%**	No loyalty at all, a shrinking market
'I might buy a shirt'	**Distant Lover – 2%**	Family used to follow club but moved away
'I used to be higher up the ladder"	**Lapsed Lover**	Might go to Cup Finals or Play-off matches
'I used to go'	**Armchair Fan**	Just watch on TV

* % of fan types at the club

out in a freezing cold December day where it is so windy the football entertainment is curtailed or b) come along in spring, summer, and autumn when the grass is green the temperatures are warmer and there is the chance of making it a far more enjoyable experience.

- Fans can travel home from away matches for a few hours of daylight rather than in a dark, wet night.
- Could give lower leagues a window to attract floating fans of other clubs if it was adopted in the SFL but not the SPL for example.,
- Far less postponements means less chance of losing money and helps reduce the uncertainty of budgeting.
- It has worked in the Scandinavian countries where they ALL have a higher co-efficient than Scottish clubs and ALL their national teams are ranked higher than the Scotland national team.
- Could revitalise the game and get more people talking about it and playing the game. The school holidays for example provides a fantastic opportunity during the 8 week period to get the community programmes working at full tilt to engage with the next generation through coaching and by bringing them into stadiums and out from under the feet of the parents.
- Better chance to get other US style marketing around the stadiums whether it be family entertainment or tailgate parties.
- Potential for more lucrative TV deals in summer.
- Clubs can secure additional overseas matches via tours etc.
- Ground maintenance costs reduced in the summer

Against it

Well there aren't that many reasons why you wouldn't consider it. Apart from tearing down the walls of our traditional routine. What we need to remember it that this very traditional schedule comes from a different era when the landscape and life in general was so different. How many other activities from the 1870s still exist in their original format?

- Would not be liked by traditionalist fans who would object; but as they are probably the most super loyal customers they would continue to attend anyway.
- It would need some thought for hospitality timings e.g. where you might have served lunch would it need to almost be replaced by a brunch. It is important that nothing interferes with this important revenue stream.

- *Some fans might miss games as games would be played during the school holidays; but the reality with the seasons getting earlier there is already a significant cross over in terms of the time of the school holidays that currently overlap with the start of the season.*
- *The traditional derby fixtures around Christmas and New Year would be lost.*
- *Players could have issues with missing family holidays in the summer. This could be accommodated with maybe time off during international weeks and of course having Christmas and New Year with family that they would not usually have. This of course could be perceived as a huge advantage by many professional players who have never had a festive season off to be with their families.*
- *How do you do a pre-season in February unless you can go abroad.*

WHAT OUR EXPERTS THINK:

Donald McGruther

If ever there was a no brainer in Scottish Football them to me this is it. I remember when I was running Falkirk, the ridiculous situation that still happens in Scottish Football when the bad weather comes in - you have nowhere to train. Even if you did find somewhere it can hardly be more than just keeping the players ticking over. It hardly works for customers - who wants to go sit in a dark, freezing February afternoon in a virtually empty stadium where the two teams try their best to entertain you (which can be hit and a miss anyway).No... let's do it, for what have we got to lose?

Bryan Jackson

From a financial perspective, I would say yes to summer football. Whilst Administrator at Motherwell and Dundee, I experienced games being postponed and rearranged which gave an immediate hit on the cash flow. Then there was the double whammy of spending time trying to rearrange the fixture where you would have a far reduced crowd on a midweek winter night. I remember seeing you (Paul Goodwin - the author) on TV during the referees strike saying that it cost you (Stirling Albion - then a Division 1 side) over £10,000 from a fixture against Thistle that was postponed. We need to protect existing revenue and look to generate new sources. I think you would bring in a new family audience with the games being played in the three seasons where we have better weather. It's Scotland, let's leave winter out!

David Mackinnon

Absolutely crucial to a re-launch and re-invigoration of the game in Scotland. As an example of how to turn your young customers against the game at an early age let me give you a tale from my days as Chief Executive at Kilmarnock:

I spent many games going to the 4 stands at Rugby Park to review the customer experience from turnstile to seat. One cold and wet December I found myself in the East Stand sitting beside a family: mum, dad and two kids aged around 4 and 6. Twenty minutes into the game with the biting wind and rain sweeping into the stand the kids started crying and collectively said "Daddy I want to go home I don't like the football" The father said "I've paid for you to watch this so you'll be staying till the end" After ten minutes of listening to the poor kids I told the father that it wasn't fair on them and I gave him his money back and promised him tickets for a game when the weather was better. If we were re-inventing the game today we would play over the summer months. Originally football steered clear of the summer months to accommodate traditional "Fair Holidays". The holiday season is now staggered so it's not relevant today and furthermore we now seem to play from June onwards to pre-qualify, unsuccessfully, for Europe so changing the season will have a huge impact on attendances, skill levels and maybe, just maybe, would see us qualifying more as we'd be in the middle of the season and not trying to get match fit in these crucial Euro games.

Jocky Scott

I think the time is now for summer football. As a coach for many years, I know the benefits of working with players in good weather. It is so difficult, especially when you are working with players in really poor conditions. It is difficult for the players and we would end up either calling it off or doing some ball work indoors, a lot of your opportunities to coach go out the window in those situations. In the other countries like Spain and Portugal where there is good weather it is easy for them to work in the techniques with their players and their kids.

In the summer time, the pitches are definitely better. And if the pitches are better, I think it would add a higher standard to our game.

It would certainly help the Scottish teams in Europe. Being involved in the qualifiers for the Champions League, the last couple of seasons teams have been up against it as they have played very few competitive games. We know as ex-players you are never at your best your first two or three games. If you are starting off early in July, none of the other teams are back training so you can't have friendly games in the build-up to European qualifiers. It would certainly help Scottish teams in Europe if we made the switch.

Nowadays when you are seated at these games in the winter, it is far too cold to enjoy the game even if there is plenty of action. You are just trying to stay warm, you don't have the inclination to get involved in the game. We have to do it!

John Blackley

Ah, I can see we really are looking at changing the things that were set in stone. Although I am a traditionalist and loved things like New Year's Day derbies and games at Christmas, I have to say that it would have been far better playing in the summer. To be honest it is not just about summer football it is about *not* playing in winter. I think players would be better prepared and in fact I would go as far as saying that we would produce better players right through the leagues if we played in Spring, Summer and Autumn. I don't think you would find many fans who would miss the terribly unpredictable weather that we often play in. So why do we continue to do it - surely we should change it? I am sure that it would get the backing of all the players and coaches.

Steven Tweed

I have no problem with summer football. I would rather have summer football. In Japan there is summer football all the way through. I think the problem is how we make one season shorter? Going straight into a summer season there does have to be two shortened seasons somewhere or at least one to balance it out.

We have had the discussion about cost, but there are 3G pitches. I think it is below -17 before they become unplayable. But there is infrastructure which clubs use, there have been hundreds of thousands spent on them, but they can't depreciate cost on them. It's not like they can be written off. They are assets and they have got them so they might as well use them. I think the point is finding out what is beneficial to get the most bums on seats and it does feel to me that it has to be summer football.

Davie Hay

There are two aspects here and they are regarding how it effect the players and the coaches in their training and also to find out if fans would want to come out in the good weather – regardless of the quality of the football in the summer time. I thought years ago that it would never work; but now I believe it is worth a try, more from a supporters point of view. It is better to coach in good weather, better for players to train in good weather, so would it be better to watch it in good weather? You are not going to need floodlights in the summer time. So is it worth trying? I think it could be, where it has got to the stage with the football that we have to look at what options are viable and are worth giving a go.

Where we should start making comparisons is with the Scandinavian countries seeing how it benefits their game. They were forced into it, it is pretty obvious, their winters are more severe there so they just close down.

I thought the Scottish Premier League looked more open last season than what it had been in recent years. The big reason for that was that Dunfermline had looked like they were always going to go down, where if you looked at previous years there was maybe four or five teams involved at least up until the split. I think we all want a competitive league and if that happens to be in the summer, then I think it would help football in this country a lot. I am just worried we don't believe in ourselves enough to make it happen.

Kevin McGoldrick

I think summer football could work at the lower levels, but it would bring its problems as well. I know, obviously, it would help playing in summer rather than winter timehowever, if you switch to summer football when do people get their holidays, especially if they are part time? I am a big convert for you being able to play anytime; because at Stenhousemuir there is the astrograss. You have to remember, pitches in the summer can dry out as well. Whereas on astrograss you can play winter and all year round. I still believe there is real potential in a revised winter break, four or six weeks in January. I do take the point though that it would be much better for fans to watch as well as players to play to a higher standard in better weather. If it happened I would not object.

Alex Smith

Let me ask you - you are a fan, do you want to sit in the freezing cold for two hours with your kids watching players do the best they can with atrocious conditions? No I didn't think so. If we were inventing football now it would never be played in winter. It started in Victorian times when folk hardly got time off any time of the year. Summer football is something that we have been talking about for years and I think we need to do it. Apart from making it a better experience for the paying public, think about the impact it would have on our players. Better training conditions, better parks, better weather will help us develop better players and a better product on the park. Yes there will be difficulties with a transition season but we would all be prepared to do that if it helps the game in the future. This is the type of legacy people in my position need to strive for, we can't sit and wait on something happening - we need to make it happen.

Des McKeown

One question you could ask is when is it summer in Scotland? There was a game cancelled in the summer at Falkirk for a waterlogged pitch and that would have been coming to middle of the season in a proposed summer league structure.

That is one of the elements as well though, when do you get your holiday season that sits with the schools? The majority of families might change now with the economic climate, most families will have certainly a week; maybe two weeks away now if you think of the proportion of your crowd that relates to they are going go away at some point during that period. I just think the biggest thing for me would how would it fit in with UEFA and FIFA competitions at the top level. If you can solve that then there is no reason why it could not work down through the league structures in Scotland.

Jamie McGowan

I know it has worked elsewhere in Europe - mostly in Scandinavia and the like. It does not seem to have done them any harm with a better qualification record with clubs in Europe and for the national teams - even in this year's Euros we had Sweden and Denmark. I know there are doubters; but so what, we need to move on as the tried and tested route is no longer working. I am all for it and I just can't see how anybody would argue against it.

Jackie McNamara

From experience again from playing in Europe, when we were at Falkirk we played against a team from Lichtenstein called Vaduz and we weren't fit. They had played so many games more than us, and if we had played them a month later we would have beat them. There is no doubt about that. When we were trying to qualify for the Champions League when I was at Celtic or getting to the next stage of the UEFA Cup it was always difficult as many of the teams we played had summer football and were up to pace rather than us just having finished a pre season.

We should try and get football moved into the summer to try and get more kids playing the game, they are the future. If you invest in them – let them in free to the games; someone is going to have to come with them. It makes perfect sense. I wouldn't want to take my kids to games in the depths of winter and I am a football man so what chance have we got of bringing in ordinary fans who might just have a passing interest in our game? I say let us do it - what have we got to lose?

Darren Jackson

It will be dry and warmer and it makes for better coaching both for players (at all levels) and for fans watching. Of course it would be hard for summer holidays so you might have to think about how you do that. I would expect most of the players would vote for it for it from a career perspective. If we don't go for summer football then I think only the SPL should have grass with leagues below on astro as it is good for developing talent. However, I am definitely not dismissing summer football as I would have preferred it as a player.

Sandy Clark

I think we should try it and the sooner the better. If you look at our game now and there are two sources of income: one is the TV and the other is supporters through the gates. When you are taking young kids to games down here, it is freezing. It is not ideal taking kids and from the fans perspective it would be a bonus to watch football in nice weather. I think TV companies would jump at it, maybe not when the World Cup is on but definitely in the summers when there are no major competitions. They would want the contract in the summer, because it gives them football 52 weeks of the year.

European countries with good weather have the benefit of training three times a day. It is not just about running but there is more of an emphasis on the technical side. Making you a better player, training 3 times a day for an hour and a half with a rest in between. Learning with the ball and making you better with it in tight areas. I think this is an issue that players, managers, coaches, physios, medics and the fans all feel it would make the game better. I hope those who make the decisions listen to the collective voice.

Conclusion

The fans want it, the players and coaches seem to want it so I think it is something we should start to do and look at is as part of the complete overhaul of the game. Yes there will be difficulties if we play in spring, summer and autumn. How do players get summer holidays, how do we have a transition season, how do we have a pre-season in winter? These are all major challenges but for our bigger clubs they could be better prepared for early rounds of European competitions and have international tours to help sell their brands. For ordinary fans and more importantly the potential new markets of women and kids we will have a far better chance of attracting them to see better footballers in better weather on better parks. We need some discussion papers on how we do it and then we just need to get on with it.

10 USING OUR TALENTED - MANAGERS / COACHES

Football is a tough game. When you are in it there is little compromise whether you are running a club from the operational side in a declining market or are a football professional with the demands that the board put on you for success on the park. If you are a professional manager or coach and you have been relieved of your position then there aren't many other vacancies in your field. Turning up at the local job centre and looking for a position just does not work for the unique group of highly trained workers, unless of course they want a career change. Football is a tough industry to get into as a coach with so much based on luck as much as skill or even being in the right place at the right time to get an appointment. So what happens to coaches or managers when they are out of football? Well nothing actually. If they are a big enough name some media work might come their way, but for the vast majority nothing happens and they drift out of the game and just throw their hat in the ring for the odd job here and there in the hope of a fresh start.

I remember sitting at an event at the Thistle Hotel in Glasgow at a fundraising dinner in memory of the late Phil O'Donnell. I had been invited by Partick Thistle director David Beattie and he sat me next to the then Thistle manager Ian McCall. Ian and I had met a few times that season when the Jags and Binos met and on his visits out to Stirling he was always coming up to cadge a cup of tea or coffee from our wee boardroom. We also knew each other from when I had been helping Thistle secure their shirt sponsorship deals and I always asked how his son Edson (named after Pele) was doing and he asked how Thistle (my son Gregor's middle name) was doing. At the dinner Ian started talking about the nuances of management and had congratulated me on getting Jocky Scott and John Blackley to become the Binos management team. Ian was high in his praise of both men as coaches. His view was that Jocky Scott was the best forwards coach Scotland has produced. He then rhymed off a host of other players/coaches/managers who agreed. Likewise he felt that John Blackley is an exceptional reader of the game and one of our best defensive coaches that Scotland has at its disposal. Paul Sturrock obviously thought so too as he had Sloop as his number 2 for many years during his travels in England.

Were Jocky and John ready to retire? No chance. Don't worry I don't want to send them into their nearest B&Q; but what I do want is Scottish Football to recognise their talents and to harness that experience to help better the game. It is insane that we have talent and experience like that and we are happy just to ignore it. This might be in this instance working with national age groups on defence or attack or helping drive football at community and youth level. There is much to do and guys like these just want to still be involved in the game that they love. Of course Jocky has now popped up again at Aberdeen as first team coach and it is Ian McCall who is out of a job. Swings and roundabouts.

It is just not the golden oldies that are stuck on the outside of the game once they are released for club duties. I am writing this section of the book just after having had a great meeting with a football man that the country is losing to Canada. Kenny Brannigan most recently coached and managed Queen of the South with some success, in a football career that even took him to the dizzy heights of the Premier League with Sheffield Wednesday. Kenny is described by others as a football nut and a coaches' coach, but he was left jobless having walked away from the Doonhamers at the end of last season. After 10 months searching the big man could find nothing in football in Scotland, which is a crying shame when you see how much passion he has for the game and how much respect he has from his fellow professionals.

We met in Glasgow's Merchant City on the day before he headed to Canada. We talked about why he felt the need to go abroad. He said to me, " I am a football coach, it is what I know and what I think I do well: but what can I do? I have been relatively successful here in Scotland and built a good reputation as a coach; but the bottom line is that I don't have a job and as far as I can see nor is there any sign of a job. The option of going to North America is one I can't turn down. It offers new experiences for me and the chance to be working full time in football on a very acceptable salary".

Another man out of the game in Scotland is Jimmy Calderwood. A man with a fantastic track record in the Scottish game and with a compelling Dutch coaching education behind him. Is he to accept at the age of 56 that he has to retire, surely not? The day before I was first scheduled to meet him he called to tell me he had accepted a short term contract with the fantastically named Go Ahead Eagles in Holland. Who recruited him? Marc Overmars, ex of Ajax, Barcelona and of course a fantastic Dutch internationalist. Jimmy Calderwood is deemed to be good enough for one of the best football nations in the world, but not for his home nation? What does that tell us about where we are with the game in our country? Surely we should be using that experience somewhere.

Use the out of work coaches to develop the game

It costs thousands of pounds to get coaches up to the A and B license standard that is now the level that most clubs are expected to attain for their manager or Head of Coaching. Through this book you will have read some of the opinions of highly regarded football figures who still have much to give. So why are they thrown on the scrapheap awaiting that call that might not come. It is crazy that we have a game where we are crying out to get more people playing and to get better standards and yet we have all this experience out doing the gardening or trying to ensure that they don't lose their golf balls on their local course.

There are two distinct areas that need to be addressed:-

If you have an A license or equivalent badge you should not be left on the shelf. There should be an automatic default setting that allows these managers/ coaches/players to get back into football and to contribute to the game that they love.

1. Former Coaches and Managers - recycling

An SFA scheme working in tandem with our league bodies and our clubs should be employed where all out of work senior license holders are redeployed back into the game. These coaches and managers like Blackley, Calderwood, Gus MacPherson, Davie Hay, Ian McCall, John Hughes and John Collins (before they took over at Livingston).

2. Former players getting young talent in to the game - given experience

So you are a big name player, maybe an ex internationalist, for example Paul Hartley who is helped into his first job at Alloa Athletic and you have a very reasonable chance of getting a start. What about those who could be fantastic coaches who don't have the name. A certain Sir Alex Ferguson starting at East Stirlingshire is a good example of how important it is to get the retired players a foothold in the coaching environment. Too often it is just down to chance i.e. where a player finishes his career and if he has any opportunity at that club.

Working with the SPFA we should offer retired players a role as they progress through their badges. Maybe it is as simple as giving them a secondary school to mentor or getting them involved in District sides at the various level in football.

How will this work?

On getting an A license badge all players/ coaches/ managers are placed on a register held by the SFA. As part of that process their employment status is noted along with their contact details. If they are out of a job they are given placement opportunities at clubs throughout Scotland at a range of different levels. For experienced coaches this allows them to remain active and part of the system.

- **mentoring up and coming managers**
- **mentoring up and coming coaches**
- **assisting coaching development**
- **assisting player development**
- **assists with high profile visits to clubs**

Funding these initiatives

- I would fund this by redistributing some of the existing funds that the SFA have available to them from the likes of the Proceeds of Crime funds.
- Create a new sponsorship opportunity where these coaches are redeployed as Stagecoach or Scottish Gas Ambassadors -

I would also turn the scheme into a campaign and use these ambassadors at all levels of the game.

For it
- *Keeps our talented coaches involved in the game where there are limited opportunities*
- *Helps develop a process of mentoring*
- *Helps Mark Wotte's strategy by having a pool of coaches who are taking his method out to the wider community*
- *Offers huge PR opportunities. Imaging the power of Jimmy Calderwood doing sessions at schools in Dunfermline or Aberdeen or helping the four or five junior clubs in Fife.*

Against it
- *Funding would need to be secured and this would require the political will from the SFA to make it happen*
- *There needs to be as much emphasis on the young pros wanting a start in coaching as there would be in the older generations*

Donald McGruther

I guess I am answering this as a fan as much as anything. It makes sense to me that that you have to use all the talent that you have at your disposal. I know it is a results driven business, but we have so much talent and I mean internationalists with 30 or 40 caps who nobody listens to. I think there has got to be a way that that talent is utilised to help the game even at Grassroots level where their status alone can help improve standards.

Bryan Jackson

There is no big picture in some of the most critical aspects of the game so interesting concepts like this will be way down the list in terms of importance. Getting the experience of the people you talk about back into football is a great way of keeping them involved and of course helping younger coaches and managers start their careers off too. I don't know how you make it happen; but I think if done properly it could have a great impact at local level.

Jocky Scott

I think if you look at the amount of managers in Scotland who are out of work and have had previous experience in coaching it is quite unbelievable. There are a lot of good managers and coaches out there doing absolutely nothing. They could definitely do something within clubs to help the game. What they learn at the coaching school is nothing compared to what they will experience with running a football club.

The biggest problem nowadays is that every chairman and director of every club regardless of what division they are in expect them to be winning the league from the start of the season. And if they are not winning the league then there is a school of thought where they will say 'let's bring another manager in, they will make a difference'. At the end of the day, yes he may make a difference in terms of the training, a difference in terms the style of play, but what he won't make a difference on is whether or not they are a good player or a bad player. You can improve them but if they can't take it on board what you are teaching them and put it into practice on a Saturday then you are up against it.

I think there is a place in the game for experienced older coaches. I believe there are too many younger managers coming in. The first thing a younger manager will do when they get a job is appoint someone they are close to as their assistant. It will most likely be someone of a similar age, or younger, and just as inexperienced. They don't think that about it from the aspect of their own inexperience and that an older coach could be beneficial to them.

I'm sure that there may be a fear that an older coach will come in and take over and start to run the place or that because they haven't any experience working with them in the past then it is too big a risk. I believe the vast majority of older coaches would have no interest in wanting to take their job, they would be more than willing to help them.

The SFA have appointed six elite coaches within their organisation to oversee six regionalised areas of the country, to take what they think are the elite players in that area. I believe those who have been appointed do not have enough experience. I think only a couple have experience of working with league clubs. They have now got the responsibility of working with these kids who they class as the elite, so they can educate them so when they are 17 they are ready to play in a first team. I think it is ill advised and I believe it was a real good opportunity for the SFA to put experienced people in those positions and they didn't do it. Experienced people know what it takes for a young kid to get to a level to play in the first team. They can also put discipline into kids in terms of how to go about their job, educate them in terms of how to play as well as learning their position within a team I have my doubts whether some of these younger coaches have enough experience in teaching the nuances of the game from a positional and tactical sense. It make sense to use us old guys who are out the game to help the game at whatever level we can help with. I would stay in the game and give something back no matter what level it would be at.

John Blackley

I think it is a good point. It not just old stagers like me. Look at the experience that Gus McPherson, Andy Watson, Billy Davis, Ian McCall have in the bag. Surely we can find a place for that in the game at whatever level. I think this is an important point. It is just not about being a 1st team manager but having a system that a wee country like us does not waste the people who have massive experience. You are only as good as the people who you have and it is wasteful not to have them engaged in the process of making the game better.

Steven Tweed

Of course it is a moot point whether the folk out of the game were any good in the first place. Having said that there is a host of talent out there that we don't tap into. Why don't the SFA ask Walter Smith to help with this project (or maybe Alex McLeish or

Owen Coyle - added the editor)

There are a host of players just retiring who can't see a pathway forward and they are being blocked too as this is just not enough positions. I think we really do need to think creatively about this and I agree we need to do something.

Davie Hay

I would say this but football is too quick to dismiss its talented people. In other industries you see people who face redundancy get help and support; but the football industry just treats you like a casualty if you finish at a club. We have far too many talented people who could be giving back. I totally agree it needs coordinated. It is not just about keeping young guys out it is looking at the whole picture where the SFA can redeploy talented guys to help their own coaching development and even leagues like the juniors, amateurs or juveniles who all could benefit from having access to that talent pool.

Getting younger coaches into the game remains an issue that also needs addressed and I see that young and old could share the same pathway in this instance.

Kevin McGoldrick

When I first started to do the coaching thing I wanted to learn the game as a coach so I went to Queens Park under14s. I was ambitious and ended up coaching the 15s, 17s and then the under19s. At Stenhousemuir I was ready to take the next step. In today's game there are so many players who will be taking their UEFA A licence while they are still playing the game and as soon as their playing career if over they are looking for a manager's job.

I think with the coaching courses, there is a sense that they are looking for people to come and give them fresh ideas. I have spoken to people within the game and I believe there is a fear factor. If there are experienced coaches assessing you, and they disagree with what I am doing there is always a chance of being judged on the basis of those coaching sessions.

Paul Hartley is a great example of a young coach who made a good decision, because he has realised there was no point in waiting for an opportunity at a first division club where the chance of not succeeding straight away is much higher. Paul Lambert is a good example of someone who, when they finished playing, made a name for himself, but only after he had had a bit of a nightmare at Livingston. He was then able to get the job at Wycombe Wanderers and the rest is history. Just as we need the wee teams to help nurture talented players it is a great starting ground for managers and coaches too - Sir Alex Ferguson and East Stirlingshire FC!

Alex Smith

I know how fortunate I am to still be gainfully employed at my age. Age brings experience and if you have learned from that experience it should be a huge help to those following you. We need to look after our managers and coaches better and help them give back as they move through the system. We also need to help bring on the young coaches from when they stop playing. I think the only way to do this is through the SFA who should use the assets they have better and maybe in doing so the game at all levels would improve. Could "the game as a whole" benefit from having Jimmy Calderwood, Gus McPherson, Billy Davies to name a few helping drive the game forward at Hampden and out around the country. Of course the answer is yes, they just need to do it.

Des McKeown

I think there is a role for these guys. However, my point would be what do they expect to get paid first of all? You talk about recycling but when these older guys go out the game there is a younger one coming into the game. So there are only so many jobs at the moment in a coaching element and the older guys who are going out of it, I'm not saying they won't get another crack at it, but they had their chance. And I am playing devil's advocate here because I do think there should be a role for these guys. I am just thinking "well you have had a chance and you've not done it."

Nationalise the youth development. There're your jobs!

Jamie McGowan

You can make an argument about the amount of coaches that are already in place, look at Falkirk, they have four coaches at the club, they have Stevie Crawford, Neil McFarlane and Alex Smith and I saw the game against Livingston and they were played off the park and they lost convincingly. John Hughes is in there on his own* and you ask yourself is there any need for so many coaches?

I would have loved to get involved in coaching but nobody asked me and I just couldn't find a place. I would still do it if an opportunity came up.

* he has now John Collins as Director of Football and Gareth Evans as Assistant Manager but at the time of the focus group he was indeed on his own. So much so that Jackie McNamara joked that he was even driving the bus - in fact he was when going to games with his U 17 Squad.

Darren Jackson

I like it. Spending time at a few clubs giving coaches a helping hand allowing them build the game from the bottom up. It is good to give them solid experience otherwise there is just no pathway and it is just down to luck if you get an opportunity. I think using your older experienced guys who can teach how to handle players and can talk about their experience at the top of the game is a great way to maximise the talent at all levels.

Sandy Clark

Younger managers are often the cheaper option. Depending where your club are at the time, it really depends on what they are looking for. I think a lot of chairman will try an experienced manager and if it doesn't work they will try an inexperienced manager for whatever reason. It's all about players. You are only as good as the players you have got. You get what you pay for.

You can't buy experience. You only get it by living in football or whatever job you are in. It is sad because there is a wealth of experience which is not being tapped into and that is why I have been doing some stuff with the SFA coaching course. There are 44 candidates coming, the majority of who are top class players. Where the hell are they going to get a job?

David Mackinnon

Football Management is very insular and full of protective traits and whilst this talent bank would undoubtedly improve skill creation it would be difficult to integrate into professional clubs with a sitting management team. Where a young manager is open to the support and guidance of an experienced ex manager, as at Falkirk where the combination of Steven Pressley and Alex Smith works well, experience has told me that this type of relationship is few and far between as the vast majority of managers see any outside advice as a threat to their authority and I know of many Club Chairman who've floated the idea being told in no uncertain manner not to interfere which inevitably leads to an acrimonious relationship sometime down the line.

I do believe though that the SFA could use ex managers more to develop their own community coaches. It happens currently in a small way but it should be developed further and with more positive PR.

It happens informally at the moment in many clubs where an experienced player is given informal coaching opportunities with the reserve or youth teams. When I was coming to the end of my career and was considering becoming a manager I offered my coaching services to a local amateur side which gave me a great starting platform in setting out teams, coaching and man management. There are many youth and amateur teams out there that would embrace a professional player coming into their set up and I believe the SFA have it in their power to formalise this type of arrangement. There is nothing like the real thing but this would be a start. The main issue in young managers not making it is down to the unrealistic targets set by some Chairman at senior clubs. Very few set out a 3 to 5 year development plan and stick to it and I have experienced very good young managers being sacked due to an irrational and weak Chairman who doesn't stick to the script and believes a change will take the pressure off him with fan reaction. This unfortunately will never change unless some rules are brought in that restrict sacking during a season but this would ultimately be challenged via freedom of employment laws.

CONCLUSION

There is exceptional talent out there not being utilised and the only people who can tap into it are the SFA. Could they help with coaching, could they help spread the knowledge down through the system as well as in the communities. There is a cost in this but maybe with a £1.00 levy on ticket prices at international matches or a £5 from every Scotland shirt sold going to a scheme we could start to use the talent that we have trained to much better effect. Other alternative sources of funding would be through the development of a sponsorship package.

11 ONE LEAGUE BODY AND A NEW LEAGUE SET UP WITH PYRAMID STRUCTURE

- NOT IN 5 YEARS, NOT IN 10 YEARS - NOW

This is another topic that links into many of the other chapters in this book and it is the biggest issue that football fans, players and managers want resolved, but yet it remains out with our reach to achieve anything. The reason why is obvious: three bodies running one game means two bodies too many in my opinion. With change afoot vested interests means that it is impossible to move this forward without a real determination. What is the most important decision facing our game in Scotland has been on the back burner for too long.

As I write this tonight (15th April) the SFA have beaten their big drum and announced to the BBC via the "sources at Hampden route" that if the SPL and SFL don't get their act together on league reconstruction then they (the SFA) would consider setting up a unified league and invite the member clubs to apply. When I heard this news I was delighted even if it was through unofficial channels. This started to maybe just show a little change in mindset probably through good leadership from Stewart Regan who has started to show some real leadership qualities to try to get this moving. Much blood was spilled over this but the SFA organising the whole shooting match should NOT be a threat - it should be the IDEAL solution.

So let's take a look back at the history to see if there any lessons that can be learned from where we came from. It is quite hard to establish where the initial desire for the Premier League came from. Scotland had just qualified for the World Cup for the first time in over 20 years and in the 1960s and 1970s our club sides had performed exceptionally well in Europe. From what I can deduce there seemed to be a concern that there were too many meaningless fixtures. I can't find any massive historical uprising from fans or indeed a major campaign by club chairmen to change things. It seems that almost a campaign of stealth led to the original breakaway.

The need to revert back to having one league body is common sense and with hindsight it seems insane that in a country the size of Scotland ever thought it could afford to pay for two administrative bodies running our game. There is a huge amount of cross over and duplication and whilst from what I have seen neither organisation has much fat in it there but there will be cost savings in a streamlined organisation and more important less chance of conflict and the self protection mentality.

League restructure has been discussed in quite some detail during the last few months. These discussions have been heightened since Rangers have been admitted to the fourth tier of Scottish football. The Glasgow giants are settling in to life in the Scottish third division after a summer of fierce debate about which league they should end up in.

There have been many different ideas about how Scottish football could thrive under a new league system. Suggestions range from a 10 team league all the way up to a 20 team top division.

One of the best potential solutions I have heard mentioned is a 16 team four tier league structure. This would allow the league to invite the six best candidates from outside league football to come and join the Scottish Football League. It would also allow the chance to set up a pyramid system below the top leagues if indeed teams from the Highland League or the Junior leagues so wanted it.

30 league games a season would allow more focus on Scotland's two cup competitions. It has been successful in the Portugal premier league as their success in European competitions in recent times shows; in the last two seasons alone Benfica made it to the UEFA Champions League quarter final, Sporting Lisbon has reached the Europe League semi final and both SC Braga and Porto have reached the final of the same competition.

It would also allow a playoff structure to be in place all the way throughout the leagues and you could work in a two up, one down, with the 15th placed team in the division facing the fifth in the league below in a play-off semi final, the third and fourth placed team in the division below could compete in the other semi final, both teams could then meet in the final to decide who goes up or who stays put.

With only one guaranteed (potentially two) to be relegated in this league structure, it takes away a lot of the pressure that many clubs claim is currently in existence due to the smaller leagues.

One thing which is almost exclusively agreed upon is the need for a playoff structure to be in place between the second tier of Scottish football and the top division. The 2011/12 campaign was a prime example of a competitive league losing its excitement in the closing stages as Ross County ran away with the title.

Sides such as Falkirk, Partick Thistle, Dundee and Hamilton Academicals would all have had plenty to play for in the final weeks as they looked to secure their playoff place. Dundee were eventually promoted taking Rangers place but there must be an opportunity for teams to gain entry to the top flight via a playoff system. It adds excitement to a league overall.

One possible benefit of a 30 game league season is the potential to reinvent the League Cup. This proposed league structure would allow the scope to develop a regional knockout section at the beginning of the campaign.

It would seem logical to arrange the home and away four team groups by location. This has benefits on many levels. It cuts travel time for teams and especially supporters, who often struggle to travel long distances midweek. You would also have derby games and local rivals locking horns which supporters always enjoy.

For example a Glasgow section could look like this. Maybe you could argue hard on Thistle and Queens Park to get out of the section; but the financial rewards would out weigh this

1. Celtic
2. Partick Thistle
3. Queens Park
4. Rangers

Each team would play each other home and away and two teams would qualify from the group stage, which could lead to a last 16 knockout stage. You could begin the League Cup in the July and play it right through to March.

Celtic is a good example for the benefits of less league fixtures, as is the case this season with their qualification in to the group stages of the Champions League, the burden of eight extra league games would be lessened and in its place six cup games which would potentially be more lucrative. As things currently stand, this would be an ideal solution to the lack of money making Old Firm games over the next three seasons.

This is turn could allow the Scottish Cup to return to its former glories. A straight knockout tournament which would be completely different from the revised league cup. Big teams play small clubs; the romance of the cup could be potentially restored which would bring more people into the game and redistribute the wealth throughout the game.

For it
- *This gives the fans what they want*
- *This give the players what they want*

- *This gives the managers and coaches what they want*
- *This helps secure a strong larger top division meaning that those top Division 1 clubs can continue with full time football which is constantly under threat as we recycle profits to ensure we do not lose this vital part of the full time structure of the game*
- *Regionalised conferences in lower leagues with play offs and pyramid scheme will stimulate the whole game and allow for the game to grow*
- *With fewer big, important games there is an opportunity to make more of these games thus increasing price and aiming for sell outs as these games become more valuable.*

Against it

- *The SPL always give us the argument that it is unaffordable due to the TV deals that are in place- our argument is that the bigger games it creates will negate that fact as will the increased revenue from these games.*

WHAT OUR EXPERTS THINK:

Donald McGruther

The SPL or the failed SPL experiment as I like to call it, is responsible in no small measure for Scottish football being on a life support system. I don't get the model- 4 games in the past brought bigger crowds these have decreased because of TV and because they are dull. They keep on talking about the "product" well it is more than that to the hard core of folk like me who still go. We are losing generations who just don't want to commit and having a negative league with repeat fixtures is a nightmare fans don't want.

We need bigger leagues - what was wrong with 18 in the not too distant past - we had great players, great teams doing well in Europe and a great national team. So what now? Accept the SPL has failed and lets go back to what worked for us.

Bryan Jackson

I would agree with one league body and a new league set up as soon as practically possible.

From what I have seen prominent figures in football such as Walter Smith and Kenny Dalglish have called for leagues of 16 or 18 and it seems the football authorities need to consider the wishes of their customers who want change. For me I hanker back to a big league where you really looked forward to the visit of big teams.

Jocky Scott

I would like to see a bigger Scottish Premier League and reconstruction in the lower leagues in a way that involves more teams being able to be promoted and a relegation system which would see teams from the East of Scotland, South of Scotland and the Highland League being involved in a pyramid system where they have an opportunity to get into the league proper. At the moment we have the Premier League and then the three divisions and team that finishes bottom of the 3rd division never gets relegated. They are the only team in the leagues that can finish bottom and have no worries and no fear. I think to make it a viable product I think we should get four full time teams to join the 12 that are there at the moment. I think to ask to get six is going to be difficult because of the standard of the first division at the moment. If they don't go that way, and increase the league I can only see those in the 1st division all becoming part-time in the near future. I don't see first division teams like Raith Rovers, Morton, Thistle or Dunfermline carrying on being full time as they can't afford it.

If you look at the Premier league at the moment, and there is one team that springs to mind and that is Motherwell. They finished 3rd in the league last year, they have had an excellent season, played a lot of good football, they have a young side who are keen and eager and are decent players. But that was only forced upon Motherwell because of finance, that they had to play youngsters and had to get rid of big earners. Other clubs had to do it as well but maybe didn't have the resources in terms of ability of young players coming through like Motherwell. If you had a 16 team league then the fear element would be taken away from them. I believe a 16 team league is the way forward. Teams would look at it in a different way. I have been involved in it with other clubs where you are going in that division, if you are challenging at the top it is great. If you are down at the bottom it is hard work. There is a lot of pressure from boardroom level if you are near the bottom of the league. The fear element is there and players definitely play with fear. Players go out there with an attitude of not losing instead of going in with the attitude of trying to win the game (don't forget that has an impact on entertainment on offer) The longer the season goes and you are not doing well the harder it becomes.

John Blackley

I grew up with the excitement of waiting for games against Celtic, Rangers and of course the Edinburgh Derby. It might have made sense to have gone for 4 games a season at the start, but not now when you have the TV dominating everything in football. You just can't have it both ways and I think if there are fewer big games they are more likely to sell out and be special again. If it means less money in the game then fine it means we do not overspend on imports and pay young local guys to get a chance in the first teams. We (the players, managers and coaches) have wanted to stop this four times a season routine for years. As the fans don't want it either I think it is time the club chairmen seriously took a look at this situation. I believe we could have a pyramid system of 4 leagues of 16 with play offs in each and there is plenty of room for ambition (think how well Ross County and Inverness Caley Thistle have done). My concern is that if we wait much longer there will be too few fans left to support the top two divisions and these are our essential core clubs that need to be full time.

Steven Tweed

A possible change to the league structure is the potential of sixteen team leagues with regionalised league below. There has to be enough movement in the leagues to make it interesting whether it's play-offs or relegation. I think one of the biggest worries is the potential in bigger leagues for teams to be playing for nothing in the middle of the table but I believe the league would be competitive enough in that situation.

I also think there has to be some regionalisation. Take Montrose for an example, they have had to travel to places like Annan Athletic and Stranraer four times a season. Surely bringing top junior sides like Auchinleck Talbot and Cumnock would be good. The same would go for team like Spartans who have been desperate to make an impact on league football in recent years.

Davie Hay

I think apart from what we think, the general consensus from the supporters it that they would like a league of 16. I think if you listen to supporters and I am sure in business they do surveys to find out what people are looking for and I would tend to think that 16 is the number that is coming from most supporters. I think you have to work round to get enough games from a financial point of view I think it would maybe give less fear of relegation. I think that could in the development of younger players as well. There are always different ideas but 16 seems to be the number that is more favourable. There could also be the potential to go back to 18 as it was when I was playing. If you look across Europe maybe apart from Switzerland we have the league with the smallest amount of teams.

I think you have got two teams in the Premier League in Ross County and Inverness Caledonian Thistle this season that weren't even in the league structure 20 years ago That definitely lends to the argument of possibly giving these teams outside of league football the opportunity to compete. It might not be ideal for every junior club but there are definitely a few of them that would be willing to give it a chance if the structure was right.

Unfortunately this is no longer something we can just chat about every few years it is no critical for the health of the game in the next 10 years that we get this fixed NOW.

Kevin McGoldrick

I think as well if you are playing against a team twice a season then it's only six points. So you might as well go out and have a go. If you play against teams four times a season you know that you might struggle, you are going to sit in and be defensive minded in these games.

So, I think the pyramid, as a whole I am all for it but I think without being disrespectful to other clubs but East Stirlingshire know they are probably going to finish near the bottom of the 3rd division and they know they are not going to get relegated but I think a pyramid system they would change. I think teams would think differently instead of having no consequence in a league if you finish bottom.

I think what you have got to remember is that the juniors play in a region, so if they are coming up to the third division, you have to address that and potentially regionalise the lowest two tiers, it makes the league more financially viable as well.

Alex Smith

I see three leagues of 16 which allows promotion and relegation and play offs in every league giving us end of season excitement. Bringing the bottom league up to 16 would allow another six clubs to come in, so that the ambitious clubs come through the pyramid structure. The instance is that they have to perform well enough, if not there is an exit strategy making this the perfect system that the SFA have spoken about in the last few years. Play offs in each league offers excitement for most clubs in the season. We have to get away from playing each other four times in a season; it is damaging our football.

I would also bring back the League Cup in sections that are localised which gives derbies home and away and helps say Celtic and Rangers by guaranteeing 4 fixtures as well as giving other smaller clubs exciting crowd pleasers. So in the central belt we could have Falkirk, East Stirling, Stirling Albion, Stenhousemuir, Alloa, Airdrie and Albion Rovers split in totwo groups with the top 2 going through to the draw at the next stage. It would add the missing fixtures as well as generating local interest and work for the TV channels as well who get bigger games. I can't emphasis enough how important it is for the development of players and to get rid of the negativity in our game to make this happen.

Des McKeown

I don't think the focus is in the right place at the moment, I don't think that's what happens. I think if you were focusing on the national team I think there be a greater identity across all the clubs to what the national team is trying to achieve.

I would go with an eighteen team top league with just one set of home and away fixtures. I would introduce the league cup sectional tournament just like it used to be as almost an extension on your pre-season and have two divisions of 16 below. I keep hearing that there are too many clubs. I don't agree – I think clubs find their level. And below the second division which is also 16, I think it is imperative that you have a pyramid system. Look at the value Ross County and Inverness Caley Thistle have brought to the set up.

One of the main worries of increasing the league size is the possibility for more meaningless games. The premier league in England is held in high regard but there are meaningless games in the league as well. There will always be meaningless games whether is a 10, 12, 14, 16, 18 team league. What you need to focus on is how you make it as competitive as possible. If it was my decision to decide the rules in an 18 team league, then I would relegate the bottom two automatically and the 3rd bottom I would put them in a play against 3rd 4th and 5th in the first division, similar to the two divisions below – very quickly there are more teams involved.

David Mackinnon

Whilst CEO at Kilmarnock I had the great pleasure of discussing this at length with Campbell Ogilvie then at Rangers and now of course President of the SFA. Campbell had spent some time developing an innovative fourteen team league format which had an exciting end of season split element that saw the bottom sides playing in a relegation and play-off mini league whilst the top six played for European places and the Championship.

This would satisfy the game aspirations of all teams and provide an exciting finale to the season. I discussed it informally with the SPL in the days of self preservation but that now is less of an issue following the Rangers situation.I It is my belief that in a country the size of Scotland this format would be ideal.

In respect of a pyramid structure and regionalisation of lower leagues I believe this would galvanise the leagues at the lower level. Having spent many an hour at SFL meetings there are two distinct levels of teams under their jurisdiction.

1. Teams with aspiration and the infrastructure to strive to the highest level. These sides

try to remain full time albeit under very tight wage structures in the hope that they eventually reach the SPL.

2. Community teams that have found their niche and are happy to play year in, year out in the lower leagues with an occasional cup windfall.

Both categories bring much to the game in Scotland and deserve great credit for maintaining their level but having spent three years at Dundee as CEO, the temptation in the group 1 category is to spend out-with their means in chasing the dream. This unfortunately happened when I left the club in 2008, leading to a second spell of Administration as the club deviated from a 3 year plan of prudency. With the Campbell Ogilvie 14 team league plan with play-offs and enhanced parachute payments the teams in group 1 can balance the books whilst still challenging.

The Community Clubs operate well within their means with some actually making a profit from the small place payments from the SPL but with teams having to make expensive league journeys to the farthest points of Scotland from their base, it is essential that geographical league reconstruction takes place. A spin off from this would be the opportunity to introduce regional play-offs for promotion and relegation which would again bring in additional revenue and more importantly give a new edge to the end of season.

Finally a pyramid system is well overdue and would create some end of season excitement at the bottom of the league structure but this must be controlled by the SFA to ensure that if teams drop out of the league there is a way back and that incoming teams adhere to the SFA licensing regulations. As I understand it this is not as easy as suggested but standards must not be compromised and the SFA should assist in funding.

Jamie McGowan

I think the second tier clubs would do well in the Premier League. The bottom six would all probably beat each other still as they do in the 1st division anyway. It would be very similar and a lot more money going to other clubs that wouldn't normally get it. I think when you see how close it is as the moment, it wouldn't be a bad idea to regionalise the lower leagues it so the fans aren't travelling to far. Given that crowds have been falling for years we are not exactly helping ourselves by asking fans in the lower leagues to travel the length and breadth of the country. So some sort of regionalisation is required to save money and to try and boost attendances.

Jackie McNamara

I think 16 is a good number if not more. I think at least that number as anything less is just a fudge. The SPL doesn't work, the first division works. Actually the lower leagues are probably more exciting because they have got the play offs. You look at the play offs in the lower divisions, full stadiums and fans that are genuinely excited, there is still something to play for beyond the season. In our league, Ross County ran away with it and the fans are coming to the games at the end of the season with no carrot for the teams or nothing to look forward to.

When Hibs got relegated to the first division the fans were out, because they were winning. You look at Hibs getting to the Scottish Cup final and I'm telling you their attendances this season have been really poor. They have a new stand and they barely fill it as fans naturally follow success. It seems obvious - if it is a fairer, more even competition you have a chance of attracting more fans.

Darren Jackson

I think it very much depends on how many games you want to play in a season. I think that so much of it depends on the TV deal, that seems to be the pre-requisite for a lot of clubs to survive in the SPL. We need a bigger league and with the bigger budgets they could compete win the league. Play offs have to be seen as an incentive and 1 up 1 down is outmoded and we need to add excitement to the game.

Sandy Clark

The first thing that you need is play-offs. I think the idea of a sixteen team league playing each other twice is not enough. It's not enough games for anybody. So if you had a split, and the top eight teams played once more, and I know you need the whole home and away thing, would it be a top six and a bottom eight, with four from the next league? I am not sure about something like that though.

I don't think you can regionalise the top two divisions. I don't think two top divisions of fourteen apiece would work. I think we need something to freshen it up and bring some excitement into it, which would give teams a chance if they are going to invest a bit of money. The play-off situation, which is great, you get a bit of extra money and in a situation like that promotion would be more of a bonus than a necessity from a financial standpoint. It is giving it a freshness and something a wee bit different. I don't know if there is a perfect solution but I think Scottish football is in agreement that something has to change.

I believe that a pyramid structure with play-off entry at a regionalised level would be very successful. I think it is important to speak to the members of the leagues such as the Highland League and East of Scotland to see if it is something their member clubs would be supportive of. One possible option is having teams entering the league structure play-off against the bottom placed team in the league - it would add a lot to the game. Teams at the bottom tier of the league would have something more to play for than just the indignation of finishing bottom of the pile.

Conclusion

How long can those who run the football bodies continue to ignore public opinion? Call them what you like but the fans, supporters, the customers want a league of 16 or 18 and to see their team play opposition home and away. If that means less revenue for the clubs then so be it, the clubs need to adjust their spending accordingly. The 16 team model with four leagues and a regionalised league cup model, play offs and a pyramid structure is what seems to be favoured by players and managers and would be more than acceptable to the fans.

12 LET'S FILL THE STADIUMS

Marketing can add value, innovate and bring in new fans

Marketing is in the main a department that does not really exist in most of our clubs, with the exception of the Old Firm, who have pretty efficient operations probably in line with Championship clubs in England. Of course most of the clubs see this vital business function as a luxury that they just can't afford which is understandable in the small market that we operate. I would argue that it is an essential that we can't afford to do without. It was interesting to read the comments of Hibs fans to the news that Fife Hyland their Managing Director had resigned from the end of this season. I was drawn to the comments on the Scotsman web site as I know Fife having worked with him years ago at an Edinburgh Marketing Agency. Apart from the various comments on ownership issues at the club there also followed the age old cry from some fans that he wasn't a fan. Then it alluded to the fact that was, heaven forbid, trying marketing activity.

I do think that this is where the league has got to step up to the plate and it really is quite shocking that neither the SPL nor SFL have a team of dedicated senior professionals advising clubs and providing best practice for the clubs. It makes perfect sense that when we have more seats empty than full that we look to innovative solutions to get bums on seats. Looking at the segmentation of the customer base and then looking at a proper competitive analysis of what football is competing against would be a start. In short the national body and the leagues don't really know the customer well enough and don't have the resource to find out. They need to see this as a vital investment to start to develop campaign marketing that adds value to existing customers, to help find new customers and try to attract them to sample the product. Innovation is clearly lacking and has been for years. It is a well-known fact that any business that is not moving forward is going backwards. Would Tesco be happy letting their stores serve the same customers year in year out or would they have a plan to get new customers in? Given that clubs don't really compete except on the park there really is no excuse for not making this a major strategic part of the football authorities plan.

In the past we have produced fantastic players not because of an excellent youth set up but due to being financially starved in many areas. Think of just how well Dundee, Motherwell and Livingston did post administration when they were forced to play young and inexperienced players. Those days are gone for the most part; however if clubs can redirect funds that they no longer require for expensive average imports, the whole scene will be better off from top to bottom. Of course the top players will head south (nothing new here) but the majority of the players will be Scottish born and bred, something they don't have in England either.

The Rangers effect this season

It has been argued that the Scottish Premier League is facing its biggest challenge in its 14 season existence after Rangers began the season in the Scottish Football League's third division. Yet with a new TV deal in place it continues to trundle along with no major shouts for help - so far.

Many have predicted that doomsday is upon us with one half of Scotland's major footballing duo playing in the fourth tier of the Scottish game. Both the SFA and SPL were quick to shout loudly that we needed to keep Rangers if not in the top league then pretty close to it (Division 1) and there was lots of behind the scenes shenanigans to try and make this happen. If it didn't happen then we were told there would be financial meltdown.

Attendances have been falling long before the Rangers situation; but there is a fear shared by many within the Scottish game that this event is the last thing Scottish football needs at the present time.

As it is topical it is worth taking a quick look at the average attendances of SPL sides from the 2011/12 campaign and compare those with the opening weeks of the 2012/13 campaign. With sides having only played a minimum of two and a maximum of three homes games it doesn't give you a full picture but the statistics do make for interesting reading. You can also factor in that the start of the season usually leads to better higher attendance figures. Weather and new season optimism usually lead in an upturn in fan attendance. There was also the promotional push for 'Sellout Saturday', a fan led initiative to get all Scottish league grounds filled on Saturday the 11th of August 2012.

With a limited amount of statistics available you have to allow for discrepancies. For example Dundee United have played two home games this season, their opening day fixture against Hibernian and their first derby against city rivals Dundee in over seven years. In both of these games you would have expected good turnouts the increase in spectators may even itself out over a longer time period.

Here are the statistics for Dundee United's attendances at the opening two home games this season compared to last

Dundee Utd home attendances   **2011/2012 - Average - 7,481**
    2012/2013 - Average - 10,402

One team who seem to be affected with a dip in attendances at the beginning the 2012/13 season is Motherwell. The Steelmen's average attendance in their first three home league games is down on last season.

Motherwell home attendances   **2011/2012 - Average - 5946**
                                2012/2013 - Average - 4360

After a 3rd place finish last season, these results are surprising and worrying. The one factor you may look at which is not explained by looking at these statistics is the fact that fans had to pay for two European qualifiers in the Champions League and Europa League respectively, which has led to games on a Sunday as well.

The side who have probably enjoyed the biggest upturn in terms of fans returning to games is Aberdeen. Their Supporters Trust was very vocal in regards to their clubs decision on whether to vote Rangers back in to the SPL

Aberdeen home attendances   **2011/2012 - Average - 9,296**
                              2012/2013 - Average - 11,756

Attendances have been impressive at Aberdeen at the start the new season and if Craig Brown's side can find their shooting boots fans will continue to keep attending games.

The examples above show that each individual club should be taken on its merits. Scottish football will most likely go through a strained and at times confusing period over the next few years and adjust to life without Rangers and the financial cuts affecting many in the top flight of Scottish football; but what might end in disaster for one club could be the making of another. Of course the Rangers crisis has meant a major change on emphasis but that is probably a good thing as we seek to reboot the game. A footnote to this story is that in conversation with one of the leaders of our game about the Fans Revolution that followed the Rangers demise he suggested that the fans hadn't lived up to their part of the deal in that they said they would turn up en masse to see games if Rangers were playing their's in the third division. This of course shows how far we are from getting a total understanding of the game at the very top. Of course fans tried, helped by Social Media and the national newspapers to get Sell out Saturday up and running and it was deemed to be quite successful. However, as I said to this official it is not the fans responsibility to market the game, that belongs to the football authorities. Otherwise, that is like asking Tesco customers to go out and find them some new customers . It just will not happen in real life so why should there be an expectation that it will happen in Scottish Football? Maybe it is because they see FANS and not customers!

There are three other major factors coming from Rangers move to the bottom of the senior Scottish Game:

1. The stranglehold that David Murray once had over the SPL when he insisted the Celtic and Rangers had a power block with the restrictive practice of needing an 11-1 vote to change anything is now history and hopefully the game will move on with a more democratic footing.

2. Rangers are now contributing to redistribute the wealth throughout the three lower leagues for the next few seasons which is helping many a wee club clear debts and get themselves onto a better financial footing and everybody agrees that is good for football.

3. The Rangers fans who were bored with the same old teams week in week out are enjoying a new lease of life and having fun wherever they go and despite the drama of finding it tougher than they thought. In short they like the escape from the drudgery of the SPL.

The marketing opportunities to change the game

There is of course the old adage that you can't flog a dead horse.

Without significant structural change, no matter what schemes you offer you will simply not be able to get enough **new** fans through the gates to justify the investment in these areas.

For the so called provincial clubs there is a dilemma in that there are football fans within their area who are only attracted to the two big successful clubs, Celtic and Rangers. I am sure that it would not take a major research paper into the psychology of the behaviours of sports fans to get to the bottom of why people want (and need) to follow successful clubs, never mind the history of the sectarian and religious issues that have blighted our game. It is important as a matter of research to understand how we used to become fans and how over the past 20 or 30 years this has changed. See Chapter no 5 where we explore the type of fans we currently have. In 2013 I will be conducting further research in this area.

I have split this section of the chapter into two; where we look at some other audiences that football has failed to attract in a major way and also look at campaigns that might also help contribute to helping saving Scottish Football.

There are three key objectives that the clubs and football authorities should be looking at and any strategies they have should be to support these basic marketing pillars:

- **get customers into the grounds**
- **get them to spend as much as possible while there**
- **build your brand by making what you offer attractive if you do that you get repeat customers**

a)The other target audiences

As we saw in Chapter 5 there are many different types of fans. However, we need to recognise the change in the demographics in the country now compared to when football was at its peak between the 1930s to the 1950s. The obvious thing to note is that football started life as a working man's sport. From works' teams to local street or district teams growing to become larger identities, our clubs morphed into bigger versions of their original self. However, just as the Labour Party found as it reinvented itself under the New Labour banner some 15 years ago to get elected they had to be seen in a different way as the working classes had shrunk and the middle classes had grown. So Messers Mandelson, Blair and Campbell knew they had to continue to play to the existing crowd (the Unions and what was left of industrial Britain) but to get elected they needed to also appeal to the middle classes. Old Labour was dumped and New Labour was born to an expectant public.

Ah the clever politicians, they knew what they were doing and managed to pull off this feat and got what they wanted out of it.

Another example of a *marketplace* in decline is the Christian Church in Scotland. You just need to look at the number of churches that have been sold in the past 25 years to see that numbers are dropping like a stone. Just stand outside any church on a Sunday and count how many people you see under the age of 30 go in. I did it at my local church and from the 50 or so in the congregation there was nobody that was obviously under the age of 30 in attendance and most disturbingly I estimated that over 50% of those in attendance were over 65 years old. I am not going to start on a Save our Churches campaign so don't worry, I will be sticking to football. There are of course very strong similarities with this audience than the football crowd. Religion probably peaked as a mass participation activity between 100 and 150 years ago. Similarly to football it has lost its way probably since the end of the Second World War. It's messaging towards the end of the last century and into this century seems so much less relevant to the mass majority and as a result it is haemorrhaging members and of course the funds that those folks bring. With less members and less money it makes the organisation less powerful and by default a lot less relevant. I think the other huge similarity is that most people in Scotland would still say that are Christians, but they don't see the need to participate apart from at weddings and funerals. If we asked lapsed lovers or TV addicts of football if they still loved football and were fans I am sure they would also answer in the same vain - the only difference being that their wedding and funerals equivalent are cup finals and play off finals.

So we can see the similarities between the organisations, however the big difference that I have seen is that the Churches have recognised that they have a problem and have over the past 10 years done significant amounts of marketing with their many campaigns from Jesus being the fisherman, fish to make Jesus your friend, etc. There have been dozens of examples of ecumenical and individual campaigns, but of course I have no idea on how successful they have been. It's not as if there has been a groundswell of opinion against the church or a massive campaign to recruit atheists it just seems to me that they have lost their relevance to the vast majority of people in modern life. Fast forward and it could be football stadiums closing down not churches in the future, as football too is less relevant (if it keeps doing the same old things). The good news in all of this is that at least it is in the entertainment industry and there are new markets that it can attract. So bringing the story back to football it is obvious that as the existing audience declines we need to find a new audience.

Families

How often has it been said that football has failed to attract families to the grounds in significant numbers. Many clubs have tried (well a wee bit) and most have failed to deliver any level of significant difference to their overall audience. What tends to happen is that a section with no swearing houses the parents and kids to compliment the parent and child combined entry fee. Is it enough? Of course not. The communication tends to be directly back to the existing audience and relates to price discounts only rather than selling the big picture. One of the most important points to note is that we know that pricing for football fans has in economic terms got inelasticity. What that means is that where football (as a whole) sits is that no matter what you do with price you can't really drive new customers into the game (there are exceptions of course).

What seems essential is to de-centralise pricing to allow clubs to target distinct groups of potential supporters. Having scope to change fixtures should be easier to do.

Scope to use price as a tool where individual targeting makes sense.

I would look at price banding with more popular games in higher bands and a sliding scale. I know it has been tried but it has not been done effectively or with the flexibility to just attract local audiences rather than having to offer the same price to everybody. The league structure throws up an conundrum . Would you want to go and see the same show four or maybe five times at the theatre? If it was exactly the same production of say Les Miserables and the top production values were guaranteed then just maybe. But you would probably be called an anorak if you wanted to see St.Johnstone v Inverness Caley Thistle five times in an eight month period. There are simply too many games and not enough fans to go around and the very notion that you keep repeating the fixtures is a shocking admission that all you are doing is milking the existing customer base.

I think we need to be taking serious stock of not just who our customers are but also of where we are losing them. *The cross border competition from the Premier League is huge and it will continue to diminish our product. What incentive is there to watch Montrose when I can relax at home and watch Man Utd. At a recent Falkirk Community Programme event I conducted a mini survey of players. There were over 120 boys in attendance and the kits they were wearing (teams the supported?) were:*

EPL	*35% (mostly top 6)*
La Liga	*25%*
Falkirk	*20%*
Scotland	8%
Celtic and Rangers	8%
other	4%

Here are some simple ideas that can be implemented ideally right across the game:-

- Buy your shopping at your Tesco (as an example) this week and get free admission for the whole family at your local team - part funded by an appropriate sponsor.
- Try Football - A national campaign where two adults and two kids can come into the game at a fixed price. This could be done on a sliding scale. The campaign could be sponsored by a commercial partner who would love the huge publicity it could generate.

A typical cost structure
SPL   £35

D1   £25
D2& D3   £20

- **The Family Card** - could be available for specific games (cup semi finals etc where attendances have plummeted in recent years) and available via Groupon as a package to neutrals after the core support have bought their tickets.

Kids-

I remember going to see Watford FC in the 80's and 90's, then in the peak of the Elton John years. It felt it as if you were at an outdoor Kindergarten with all the songs sung in tiny little squeaky voices.

A few clubs have started to look at this potential and maybe surprisingly Rangers have tried that bit harder than most and have events activities and competitions at most match days for kids at the Broamloan Road Stand.

The Scottish Terrier Club (or another name like this)

A national club where kids can join online and they get offers directed to them and newsletters that are all generic and yet can be tailored to their needs.

- gets kids playing in their community via their local club
- promotes the sport and health and well-being message
- delivered to every school in Scotland, building the game up from the grassroots
- kids go free to every club they nominate home or away up to the age of 12 when accompanied by a paying adult

Students-

Nearly every club has a further education establishment near to their ground. This is another untapped market that can help fill empty grounds with a noisy vociferous bunch.

Clubs should be doing deals with the local educational establishments and there is of course the opportunity to bring in these valuable assets (students) to help in commercial areas / in areas relating to their course work too.

Players

Lots of younger fans can't go to games as they play on a Saturday. These are real football enthusiasts. Give them tickets for midweek matches. This might be facilitated through the SFA player registration database as a way to help from to get the crowds up.

Other sports fans

We have to recognise that getting any new fans, apart from the young, is going to be difficult as we are in a very competitive market place. "What do you fancy doing: cinema in the warm or freezing yourself to death at the footie?" We have to change the fundamentals first but once we have done that then we might just have a chance of getting more people into the grounds.

Rugby has started to get its act together in schools by working with local clubs offering free training and deals. It is another way to attract an audience and you would imagine that people who are sports fans are a far better target than non sports fans. Offers to golf clubs, bowling clubs etc to get members interested in the game.

Tourists & visitors to our country

If we go back to the very start of this book and I talk about the "wee ba" that is in the Smith Museum in Stirling that shows we were at the epicentre of the origins of the game. Let's tie into the origins and entice fans to the Hampden Museum and then to take in some games. Of course if we had summer football we'd have another potential audience of many millions to attack. At the moment we haven't even a clue who our audience is.

Here are the latest figures from the GB Tourist Survey of 2011 for Scotland: £3billion spent in Scotland that equates to 44 million bed nights that is an equivalent of over 11 million trips in a year. Most of these of course come in the summer months.

Fans of other clubs

A target market that is not that hard to find- they love football are in the same league as you and you have direct access to them via the clubs.

Away fans-

- Kids go free scheme for all clubs in Scotland promoted by the SFA who reward each entry with a £2.00 fee paid out of a central pot.
- Matches becoming local events where home clubs have a suite of marketing tools to try and attract fans of other clubs to make the journey and maybe be the only away game they go to each year. Special offers at the game, local hotels, bars etc.

Pensioners (lapsed lovers)

Pensioner Saturday admission to your local club for just £100 promoted throughout the country and backed by a sponsor.

b) joined up campaigns

I have been working in football for years and it saddens me when I ask "punters" about campaigns that are out there and they look at me as if I was mad. Recently we had a *"focus on football"* campaign and I asked over 100 fans on Twitter if they knew what it was about. I am sorry to say that less that 10% had any idea about the objectives of the campaign.

Play for the jersey

I mention this campaign which I called "So you think you are good enough?", when I was at Stirling Albion as a way to demonstrate how stale we are in the game and why it pays to think just a little bit out of the box. Jocky Scott is one of our contributors asked me when he was the manager if he could go on a preseason tour to the Highlands. I told him we had no money and couldn't afford it BUT I had tested this campaign the year before and if he was up for it I would do it again. "So you think your good enough?" was just a football x-factor. Players lapped it up and we had over 100 wanting to participate. For me I used the clubs assets (coaching staff, its manager's credibility, our park and our previous unique marketing and PR appeal to make it work). With a £10,000 profit Jocky got his mini pre season trip and he also signed two players from it. This just demonstrates the most basic of marketing get results and the media coverage it created made our two main sponsors - Prudential and The Doubletree Dunblane Hotel - very happy. I am amazed that nobody copied it this year. What it shows is that it is not that hard to be different or to be creative and it just takes the desire to do it. Likewise with looking at the potential for developing bigger robust campaigns.

Reward loyalty

- If there was a Tesco Club card or Nectar Card for football fans it really would really help deliver the vast buying power that all these fans have. If you allied that to the need and desire to fill the stadiums (back to the key objectives above) then you could have a serious plan that is measureable. When have we seen clubs utilise the likes of Groupon to drive the sales of seats?

Social media can be your platform - it is not the solution

- Having 10,000 likes on Facebook does not drive your engagement nor does it demonstrate that you have done your job. The performance of our clubs in the Social Media sphere is not very good. So many likes mean nothing until they are turned into a purchase of some sort. What the social media channels offer you is an opportunity to communicate with your audience and an even wider (interested - likes on Face book etc) audience at virtually no cost. So that is great: no print, distribution or advertising costs so you can devote more margin to developing innovative offers.

Talk differently to potential sponsors -Travel offers

Ok the sponsorship market is not performing very well; but as I found out when I was working with Gordon Smith when he was CEO at the SFA is it often not who you ask but what you ask and how you ask it. In that instant the SFA were looking for a Scottish Cup sponsor. The year before Gordon engaged me to work on the project I looked at all the sponsors in the market. One of the first I talked to was Tesco who had previously been sent a PowerPoint presentation by the SFA. It looked good, but was just saying look at us we are great and look what we have, do you want it? It never got past first base. Instead I met Tesco 6 or 7 times and worked out what they were trying to do in Scotland and then worked on how the SFA could help them. Just a different tact being intuitive and creative lead to a £1million deal being signed when Tesco passed it on to Tesco Bank. It was sods law that Gordon Smith got shown the door and I never even got a thank you for my effort never mind the commission I had been promised!

So with that innovation and creativity could we not approach Stagecoach or First Group and look to get more fans travelling to away matches with special fans transport deals? Could we not hit the CSR (Corporate Social Responsibility) budgets that now exist and develop some compelling community programmes that are worth sponsoring?

VAT free for football

The McLeish Report suggested many structural ways that the game could be improved and one of the stumbling blocks that it correctly identified was the lack of funding. When I was at Stirling Albion it came as a real shock to me that 20% of my revenue headed in the direction of the tax man and yet here was a community club that would never be making a profit. So when we charged £15 on match day we were only getting £12 into the kitty.

It struck me that collectively there should be a **VAT free for football campaign** that would ring fence this money and that that 20% of gate money could automatically be put into the clubs community development pot or into a national football community development pot where the funds are used to develop infrastructure. It is measurable as all attendances are measured by the Leagues and the campaign is scalable across all clubs and of course games with the national bodies. This could galvanise clubs in a common cause and provide a way of football helping funding new infrastructure projects itself in the years to come. It would certainly create a stir and get the politicians talking.

The annual football lottery

As I mentioned football should be led not just in matters of governance, but also in areas such as marketing. I believe there is scope to develop a National Football Lottery to help the funding shortfalls that were highlighted in the McLeish Report. This could be pushed by all out football bodies be available at clubs and the money generated reinvested back into infrastructure and community projects. There would also be scope to work with the likes of Camelot who are always open to new suggestions.

WHAT OUR EXPERTS THINK:

Donald McGruther

We are a small country with limited resources and we all know and accept our limitations; but you just need to look abroad whether it is to the USA or even in Europe to the likes of Germany to see that we are just not at the races. The culture in these countries would just not allow the current status quo that we have here to exist. Oh the Taylor report meant massive investment in the structures but unfortunately there was no new thinking that went with the shiny new stadiums.

Bryan Jackson

We are stuck in a time warp in Scotland and have failed to see that with competition from other pursuits and leisure activities means that football has to work at getting fans to come. With the product deteriorating, it is even more important that marketing ideas are implemented that attract supporters who I believe are often taken for granted. I think this is partly because if for example you are a Motherwell fan, then you will always be a Motherwell fan, but that does not mean that you will not be looking for value for money. Whilst I appreciate that many clubs do not have huge resources, I do not believe that enough effort is made to bring people into the grounds.

Jocky Scott

I don't know anything about Marketing at all. What I can tell you is that we are not offering value for money for what we have on the park and because we have too few teams in the league it is boring. It is boring for players, boring for officials, boring for managers and coaches and it is boring for fans. And what have you got if you have the match on TV to incentivise anybody to come in watch it live.

John Blackley

I think it starts with the league structure and the fact we don't have the quality of players coming through any more. So I think the product on offer is not good enough and there are so many things for folk to do that it is becoming an impossible task. Once you change all these structural things then you might have a chance to get more people into the grounds. Until then I just can't see it happening

Steven Tweed

We don't have any idea in Scotland. Look abroad to places like Germany where they have joined up thinking with integrated travel and match ticketing making it easier for the customers to attend games home and away. Every season we have fans out of pocket with last minute postponements costing them time and money. There is never any apology or money back for travel – football is brutal there is no other industry that would do this to its customers and expect then to keep turning up. Marketing – we certainly need it once we get the product right.

Davie Hay

I have never thought that we do enough to get supporters into the grounds. We just rely on the fact they always come. I am not sure that will last forever. We need to make the focus on getting the whole family into football just as they do in America. Not only does that mean we get more people through the turnstiles it also means that you get more longer term followers and more revenue too. Clubs have tried wee bits and pieces with dropping prices here and there but apart from that you just don't see anything happening which is a real shame.

Kevin McGoldrick

I think it is hard for the smaller clubs to do things as they just don't have the resources or the skills to do much about the problems. I think we need to have help across all clubs coming from the SFA and the leagues to try to have an industry solution to the problem.

Alex Smith

We have to look at the big picture. Get bigger leagues, better facilities, summer football and then you can start doing all your marketing and you just might have a chance.

Empty seats – fill up the stadiums get the kids in free that way you get them into the habit of going to the games. All season ticket holders get a reduced price at the turnstile at other grounds to encourage them to go to other clubs as we are all part of the one football family

Old firm season ticket holders– give them access to reduced prices too at other grounds (maybe their local ground) when they are away from home why not encourage them to come to other games as you have 45,000 fans doing nothing on a Saturday. Maybe a special gate where you show your own club's season ticket and you get a concession ticket at the same price as the club they are visiting.

We should be learning from other businesses such as the supermarkets who know how to attract customers. The normal season ticket, why not make it a loyalty card that can be used across Scotland.

Brian Rice

Yes we should be shouting from the roof tops. Think about all the free advertising and promotion we get in the media and yet we don't do anything with it. We could do all sorts of things as we have the communications to tell people. However, we need a decent competitive league, summer football with young local talent playing their hearts out. That would give you a chance.

Des McKeown

We don't even try, do we? We are stuck in a time warp where fans are expected just to turn up give over their money and accept just what is on offer. We all agree that what is on offer is not good enough so how the hell do you market such a flawed product, I don't know? I know if there was something wrong in my business I would just fix it and fast - shame football does not do the same. Maybe once you get the basics right then you will be able to get more people back; but once you lose them it is virtually impossible. We are talking about lost generations, aren't we.

David Mackinnon

In my mind summer football will have the biggest impact on attendances, but if it is introduced all aspects of making the game more attractive and affordable must be included. I believe that with proper marketing and initiatives a new dawn would re-align the game to a new and bigger audience. In order to do so we need leadership at the top with people with genuine agendas and get rid of some of the mediocrity that exists within the power circles of the game in Scotland. At the moment there is no common agenda resulting in the on-going fragmentation of the game.

My message is leave your self-interest at the door and collectively we can provide a stable platform for a blossoming game that we can be proud of.

Jamie McGowan

I don't think clubs have the expertise to do things the way that maybe other industries do them. I think there has got to be more effort to try and get kids and families involved. Of course the problem is how do you do that when clubs such as Falkirk or Morton or the like are counting every penny and would see it as lost revenue. It has got to be a lot more considered and businesslike.

Jackie McNamara

We have done brilliantly at Thistle with kids go free and I think doing simple stuff like that is a great start; but we have such a long way to go. I am shocked that after 3 years I have still not seen other clubs copy it. There are so many other things that you can do and I think that we (the football industry) just forget that. We are so close to it because football is part of our DNA. It used to be for so many other folk too but they have just drifted away for one reason or another. The sad thing is that we have just accepted it. That is what we should have the League and SFA doing for us.

Darren Jackson

We tend to leave it to individual clubs and in my experience there are not that many that know much about sales and marketing. Maybe a national conference having everybody represented as a national football forum would be a good way of getting all the best ideas out and shared across football. I don't think we listen to each other very well. I think it is important that we all work together and of course build the game up rather than talking it down which is all done so easily.

CONCLUSION

With a proper brief from the football authorities we could have some innovative campaigns going in no time at all. Nobody seems to think we have the perfect product and everybody I spoke to agrees there is much that can be done; but we need the three bodies to embrace change, recognise the problems and work together to find solutions. I for one am happy to work with them on any of these concepts and to develop a range of other solutions that might help a) change perceptions b) get the game in the public spotlight for the right reasons c) have some campaign objectives that leads to building the football brand in Scotland.

13 FOOTBALL IN THE COMMUNITY

There are many examples of clubs now starting to realise that if they are to survive then they need to play a bigger role within the community that they operate in. I think there are a lot of examples of clubs going down that route, but trying to get a figure on it of how successful it is, it is all anecdotal. Most recently I was working with Falkirk and their community programme. It is that kind of thing that has won a number of awards over the years and they say "The Falkirk programme is fantastic", but they have never evaluated it or monitored it or asked the parents. In actual fact, and it just blew me away when we were sitting talking about the Falkirk programme, it actually has the same turnover as Stirling Albion does as a club. Because of the outreach programme and providing a service that the community needs. It make the club an even stronger part of the local culture. As I write this Stenhousemuir have just won an award for being the best community club in Scotland which is great that the value of this work is starting to be recognised. I recently spent some time at Everton looking at their Community Department activity and was blown away with how they had developed this strategy to be truly ground breaking. With links to prisons working on the rehabilitation of offenders, in health and welfare sector tacking big issues such as obesity, drug and alcohol dependency and helping to create employment opportunities. They see the benefit of working with many stakeholders and in the education sphere have relationships with colleges and universities and this in some measure has led to them becoming the first football club in the world who will open up a school through the UK Governments schools policy.

Everton Football Club has become the first Premier League club in the country to be granted government permission to open a Free School. The government-funded Everton in the Community Free School will be run by the club's charity and it opens in September 2012.

It is expected to provide education and sports tuition for up to 200 14 to 19-year-olds within three years. Its approval was announced in the House of Commons by Education Secretary Michael Gove.

Everton FC chief executive Robert Elstone said: "We have played a huge part in the Liverpool and Merseyside community for over 100 years and this latest move demonstrates our desire to continue to make a difference where it counts."

Everton FC manager David Moyes added: "It will, unquestionably, provide a real chance for some less-privileged, less-fortunate children to embrace and benefit from a high-quality education."

Integration at that level is pretty unique but what it does is show the level of integration that the club wants in the community. Most clubs in Scotland have started to embrace the community opportunity as the very obvious benefits are getting closer to the potential audience and converting them to become fans as well as utilising the stadium and other team assets in a more productive way.

WHAT OUR EXPERTS THINK:

Donald McGruther
For too long clubs didn't seem to think that giving back to the communities that they operated in was anything they should consider. Maybe the development in recent years of Corporate Social Responsibility into the commercial landscape has ensured that it is being taken more seriously now. That has got to be a positive step.

Bryan Jackson
Football has unsurprisingly not done too well in this environment over the years, which maybe reflects on how they have seen themselves in the past. Of course there is an issue here in regards to the scale of the operations that football clubs have and the capacity they have to embrace this. I see a lot of positive noises in this area with our smaller clubs but there is much to do to make this become second nature to them.

Jocky Scott
In my early days in football, the club were just a focal point for the community on a Saturday at 3 o'clock. Things have changed so much since those days and clubs need to be far closer to their fans who after all are our customers. I think that getting into schools is the key for clubs and there is a big gap there given what has happened to schools football in recent years.

John Blackley
I think this is far easier said than done, given the budgets that the clubs have to work with. Having said that I know clubs can access funds to do a lot of this work and it forges the links between club and fans which is needed now when the football business is competing against so many other entertainments.

Steven Tweed

I think that there are some good examples in Scotland of this; but compared to how it is done abroad we are miles behind where we should be in developing our community links. Provincial clubs often complain about the buses that leave their towns to go follow Celtic and Rangers and I think working in the community is partly the answer to that. If you are in the local community contributing and adding value it is hard to be ignored.

Davie Hay

It used to be that the bigger the club the less likely it was to see this working. However, I think this has been changing over the years and clubs now seem to see the value in investing in this area. It certainly seems to me that the smaller clubs identified the need to do this and that our bigger clubs have now caught on that it is the right thing to do. Without doubt this will be a vital part of football in Scotland in the future and an area that will definitely be in the spotlight.

Kevin McGoldrick

I know at my club Stenhousemuir there is an emphasis to involve ourselves with local schools. It's not just football it's also about healthy eating and helping them get involved in the facilities we have on offer in terms of our astrograss pitch. Sometimes before training we are waiting to get on for our warm-up and the kids are still on the pitch and that is great to see. So on a Saturday morning there are 100s of kids from the local schools or wherever they are coming from and they hang about when they have finished, so they are as well coming to the game. It seems to be working as well, from a financial aspect with the 5 a-sides there are teams waiting to come on after us training. I think having an active community is vital for a provincial football club.

Alex Smith

Let's be honest about it clubs have not done this well in days gone by. They just didn't see the value of it and that has been proven to be wrong, as it can bring clubs so much closer to the fan base and offer something back to the community they operate in. I am really encouraged by this positive change in football and I am sure it is a great way of protecting clubs for the future generations. I would suggest that to try and encourage this there should be more incentives / rewards for success from the League and SFA.

Des McKeown

Without doubt a real plus for Scottish football in a landscape where we don't see much positivity. We need to be up close to our audience (the fans) and there are many brilliant examples of how this has been done to good effect. I think the clubs now get it – that they can be a key part of the community – and that will bring not just good PR- but also help make fans of the future.

David Mackinnon

It is a key component of the modern club and has required a mindset change over the years. I don't think we can get complacent as there is still much to do.

Jamie McGowan

Again look at the success of the likes of my old club Falkirk in this respect. It is more than just doing coaching in the community it is using the stadium, the assets the club has and getting out there to offer services and activities that the community needs. I think there is still much to do in this area and it is vital work for the clubs to do to service in the long term.

Jackie McNamara

It is something we take very seriously at Partick Thistle and I think it is more than just building community relationships and offering coaches etc. I see it as being part of the fabric of the club and a way to engage with fans old and new in the community. I know that there will be far more investment in this area in years to come and I am sure it will benefit the club.

Darren Jackson

We tend to leave it to individual clubs and in my experience there are not that many that know much about sales and marketing. Maybe a national conference having everybody represented as a national football forum would be a good way of getting all the best ideas out and shared across football. I don't think we listen to each other very well. I think it is important that we all work together and of course build the game up rather than talking it down which is all done so easily.

Sandy Clark

More and more clubs are looking to maximise opportunities working with their community. The biggest challenge is trying to keep fans, especially young fans. In my day there was no competition. It was only football on a Saturday for young men. Nowadays you have football on the television, computer games, other sports, hobbies and activities. We now have to fight our corner. We have to go around the community and give them something that attracts them and keeps them coming to the club. At bigger clubs there is a different kind of situation although I am sure they are still finding it difficult in attracting new supporters. There is no divine right that young kids are just going to come to the football. You have to work at it and make sure when they come along that they enjoy it, whether it is playing it or watching. Once you get them there then it is up the club to keep them coming back through entertainment on and off the pitch.

There is also the fallacy now that young players playing now have a lot of money. It's nothing like that. I spoke to a first division football manager recently and their team was in the Premier League not that long ago and some of his players in his first team are getting as little as £150 per week and that is full-time. Fans probably think they are driving around in a fancy cars but in reality they probably getting the bus and the train on the way to training! So it is not the glamour thing that it is perceived to be. I know at the top end it is much different; but that is not in touch with the real world. It's not like that anymore.

CONCLUSION

We don't have any significant community marketing in Scottish football in any joined up way. Celtic and Rangers do have a professional resource as you would expect due to their size. The rest of the clubs tend to have commercial teams who survive by selling the obvious and who can blame them (trackside and programme ads and hospitality). Rarely do we see the commercial and community opportunities come together in any significant way yet there are huge long term benefits to be gained by clubs and in the short term many funding opportunities to help them get there.

There are so many good people out there; but not with the level of creativity or support that would allow them to deliver any significant returns. These initiatives need to be driven by ALL the bodies at Hampden Park with incentives and rewards as well as disseminating best practice.

14 DRAFT SYSTEM ALL PLAYERS UNDER SIGNED TO THE SFA NOT A CLUB

I n this chapter I am going to examine the possibility of taking the best aspects of American scholarship programmes and the draft system and apply it to Scottish football.

The American model of scholarships and drafts, is it feasible in Scotland?

Coming through a scholarship programme and then moving on to the professional ranks through a draft system has long been the way for developing talented young players in America. Their top three sports of basketball, baseball and American football all recruit new players in to their respective leagues after the players have served their apprenticeship at one of the many top universities in America. Players are developed through a scholarship programme. Their fees at university or college as it is more commonly referred are paid for and they have to take a major in a subject to go along with their sporting degree. These young players usually attend for four years (Freshman, Sophomore, Junior, Senior) before moving on to the professional ranks.

There is a perception that this style of player recruitment is very much America's way of doing things and that it would be difficult to adapt to another country. Major League Soccer (MLS) is beginning to establish itself as a serious challenger to ice hockey's NHL as America's fourth sport of choice. Their ability to recruit players such as David Beckham, Thierry Henry and strong showings from both the men and women's national teams in recent times have boosted the popularity of the sport. The draft system is also in place for the MLS but development is needed on that front. Football, or soccer as it is commonly referred to in the States, is the most popular game with children up until the age of 12. The problem is after that when full contact sports like American football take over and little league softball turns in to the more physically demanding baseball. Without doubt, soccer is losing the vast majority of well-rounded teenagers to other sports. The one thing that a draft system in Scotland would not suffer from is losing talented young players, as for most young men, football is the be all and end all as far as their sporting ambitions go.

The question is, could it work in this country and more importantly, how would it work? A national training centre has been mooted in the past, where all young players train and learn the game. One of the possible downfalls of such a system is a lack of competiveness, young players could potentially become almost robotic as they learn and learn some more without testing themselves.

The main concern with a national football academy is that when players have served their apprenticeship they have not been exposed to the rigors of Scottish football. If you are teaching young players technical drills and preaching the merits of working with the ball, it could be quite the culture shock for a player being thrust in at lower league football. The hope would be that eventually all these young players would have been developed in a way which would lead to a change in style in this country.

One of the other possibilities is potentially developing young players at university level. A scholarship system could be put in place where they could compete against each other while still being able to complete their education. The University of Stirling, Scotland's University for sporting excellence, has already developed a scholarship programme with its first XI football team. The side have enjoyed tremendous success since bringing the scholarship system in to place. They have swept all before them in the last two seasons, winning the British University league and cup as well as winning the East of Scotland league, beating a highly experienced Spartans side to the title. The university side have recruited players from Blackburn, Gillingham, Cardiff City and as far afield as Swiss side Basle in recent seasons. The potential of offering young players an education and a high standard of football has proved to be a winning combination for the side who are now managed by former Falkirk manager Eddie May. It is hard to argue with the recent success of Stirling, however as only Loughborough University can currently compete financially and offer players a scholarship, you would have to believe that it would take a vast sum of money to put in place such a structure throughout Scotland or even Britain. Ex University of Stirling players have managed to find league clubs in recent times, namely Danny Denholm who is with Forfar and Sam Filler who is at Stirling Albion.

University level football has its merits but one of the potential problems is that you couldn't guarantee that these young players would then want to go and play part-time football in Scotland. Their education may have already opened doors for potential careers. Also if other sides tapped in to the success of how Stirling have succeeded recently, they may well want to go down the route of recruiting players from outside Scotland. A draft process from that position could be rendered meaningless if the opportunity itself is not appealing enough for young footballers.

One potential way of working a development strategy is for young players to serve an apprenticeship and then go in to league football in a regionalised league system. You could potentially have 16 to 24 teams in place, and split the league in to sections by location.

As I touched on in one of my previous chapters, this is a way you could encourage our talented managers back in to the game. The benefits of this would be by getting these coaches back in to work. They would be able to give these young players advice of what is in store if and when they make the step up. Even if the ex-manager was just a figurehead or there in a mentoring capacity to coach up or give no nonsense advice, then there surely would be some benefit in that. One of the criticisms raised in regards to national training centres is it is full of coaches who have studied the game, but have not played or coached at the top. These young coaches may have the qualifications but I believe ex-managers on the whole have that inherent ability to deal with each player as an individual.

In the hope of translating the successful draft/recruitment system from America to Scotland, there has to be room for adaptability. Typically players in America spend their development years in education/scholarship from the age of 18-22 if they do not declare early. This would be less feasible in this country when it comes to football as players here develop much earlier than that. Almost exclusively young players will sign on at a football club after completing their fourth year of high school. Most will be either 15 or 16 when that happens. If you were going to develop a regional league, you would imagine that these players would have to come in whilst they were of a similar age or their development could be severely hindered.

One of the real benefits from a potential scholarship system working better in Scotland than across the pond is there would be no 'big man on campus' attitude. These young players would be brought in and be provided with food and accommodation but their development would be very much out of the spotlight. There would obviously be some form of media attention if such a project was successful but these young players would be subjected to scrutiny from potential employers rather than the tabloids.

Some college players in sports such as basketball and American football are watched by millions on television and thousands in stadiums each week. Their decision to stay in college or declare themselves eligible for the draft, literally could cost them millions of pounds if they come out a year too early or stay in college a year too long. If the scholarship programme was successful in this country, these pressures would not apply. They would be allowed to develop for the most part behind closed doors.

To look at how players would actually be drafted in to the league it is easier if we take a particular sports draft to examine. The National Football League draft system is relatively straightforward and provides parity to a league which is often regarded as the most competitive and smoothly run of all the big American sports.

In the NFL there are currently 32 teams. The structure for their draft which takes place in the off season each April is as follows.

The team who finished last during the regular season picks first in each round. The Super Bowl champions pick last in each round. Each team is placed in order of their success in the previous season. This enables teams who struggled the year previous to pick elite talents to help re-build. A salary cap is in place already but it helps to add to the competitiveness of the overall league.

So here is an example of how it could potentially work in Scotland if you bring in a similar system to that of the NFL.

If you use last season's standings from the SPL all the way down to the SFL Division 3, it would look like this at the top and bottom of a potential draft.

1. East Stirlingshire
2. Clyde
3. Montrose

40. Motherwell
41. Rangers (Although beginning in SFL3 complicates this)
42. Celtic

There is obviously some room for debate on how the structure would actually work if it was put in to practice. There is some doubt if it would be both an SPL/SFL joint venture or if it would be more beneficial running solely as an SFL product.

If such a system was put in place it would undoubtedly save some of the bigger clubs, who are currently investing heavily in youth. It would then allow them to focus much needed finances in other areas.

You could argue it could be a hindrance to clubs like Falkirk, Partick Thistle and Hamilton who have worked hard in developing their youth setup, but a potential overhaul of youth football in this country would surely have more positives than negatives.

There would also have to be a strict wage structure in place for the first two years of the contract. These players would obviously not be able to make top youth prospect money at a part-time third division club. An agreement would have to be in place between the clubs and the governing bodies and you could also look in to getting these wages part funded in some capacity.

Every player drafted could sign a two-year deal with their club and if they are successful the club will be owed a set-price £50,000 once they move on. This would be a way for clubs to bring in real money to help them prosper in the long-term. The main downside to that may well be if a first division team had developed a talented player who could easily command a bigger transfer fee, then a set fee would be a hindrance but the constant regeneration of money back in to clubs would arguably outweigh any particular grievances with singular transfers.

Going back to the premise of bringing in experienced coaches who find themselves out of the game for whatever reason, would be invaluable given their experience but there also has to be the balance of new-era coaching and making the most of new technology.

If potential regional development areas were put in place, it would allow young coaches and wily old managers to work together in developing their regional side.

You would also end up having young players being recruited by each regional team before they arrive. Each regional side would have something to offer: location, type of football played, potential opportunities for game time and the incumbent manager's previous track record of developing young players in the past.

The follow on from that could be the recruitment policy of SFL/SPL teams during the draft, certain teams may like the style of players, for example, that Jocky Scott develops, others may prefer Jimmy Calderwood players. These type of tactics along with positional value would surely become an interesting sub-plot in the lead up to a draft.

There is also the opportunity of potential draft day moves or trades as they are commonly referred to. In the NFL players already on rosters can be traded for potential draft picks, that again would be something to potentially look at as it could be achievable.

For example if we look at last season again, Celtic (Pick 42) could offer East Stirlingshire (Pick 1) three of their promising under-19 players on a season long loan and their first round draft pick for the next three seasons to trade up and get the best player coming out of the regional leagues that season. If Celtic felt that the best player could improve their team, it would allow them to move up and get that player, while suitably compensating East Stirling in a way which most likely would suit them in the short and long term.

This idea more than any other in this book would take a lot of things to work. If Scottish football is looking for real change and to put in a system which would require patience and may take a number of years to reap the benefits but the rewards ultimately could be something special then this should be seriously considered. A working system which eventually would provide Scottish football with young talented players moving forward in a sustainable manner.

<u>WHAT OUR EXPERTS THINK:</u>

Jocky Scott

The biggest problem that we would face in our country is that we have never done anything like that. In America they have grown up with that, every sport does it. Basketball, baseball, soccer, American football is all done from a draft coming from college players. So they do that, even in MLS the league owns the registry of the players.

Where do they SFA or the league get these players from? The facilities, infrastructure and coaches that are in place in the United States are second to none. So by the time the kid is leaving and he is going into the draft system he is well established as a player. So they go from a college, then they go in to the draft, then they go into a club. I query how the SFL and SFA would be able to put such a system in place in Scotland.

John Blackley

I like the idea of nurturing talent centrally as they have done successfully in France and Spain and I like the idea of getting more talent into the system. Of course this would also help us become far more competitive too. However, it is far too radical for Scotland and it could never work as who would vote for it? Maybe if we just had the one body(SFA) organising this then it might have a chance and it might work but there is even little chance of that happening.

Steven Tweed

My son is nine and he has been asked to go and play for clubs in Glasgow and there is no way that I will let him. In two years he might not be good enough and he might not want it. But from an early age these days, they are being released. They are getting told they are not good enough, there is a strong chance by the age of eleven that they have already been let go by one of the bigger clubs and told that they won't make it due to their size. It is unbelievable and I think we do need a radical overall of the whole youth set up. I think the Mark Wotte appointment is a step in the right direction but we are so far behind it is leaps we need to make, not steps!

Davie Hay

I know the American system well and it generates a huge amount of excitement across all the sports not just in soccer. I like the idea of doing something different, but I feel it would need to be part of a far bigger plan and that is probably another book you need to write.

Kevin McGoldrick

I like the idea but I think that it is far too radical for implementation in Scotland at the moment. I think the important thing is that we start to talk about these things and that there is a debate about the merits.

Alex Smith

I think it is a big radical thought and could not be done in isolation and to be honest I can't see anything like this ever getting considered which is wrong. Again, we have to be open to look at the whole picture. The problem is that there is reluctance to change and too many vested interests. To me things like this are worth talking about as we look to reshape the whole game. The thing is it should not be done in isolation. We are in a serious situation where Panama, Cape Verde Islands and the Central African Republic are all ahead of us in the World Rankings. We as a nation should be having a big debate about ALL our options NOW and with all the stakeholders involved in our game.

Des McKeown

Up to the age of sixteen the SFA should develop every single player. How do Celtic and Rangers buy into that? I'll tell you why they should buy into that because at 16 or 17 they are having to buy from other clubs anyway because the vast majority of their players aren't going to make it into the first team. They then go and buy the best from other clubs. The SFA should develop every player then it should go to a paid draft system. And I thought about this myself, I don't think you can stipulate that the best player in that system goes to the bottom club as the way it is done in American sports.

I am not talking about an elite group of players to begin with. I am talking about every kid and it might be certain ones promoted over the course of that period to an elite group, a community group whatever that may be. My fear is that every single club has jersey fillers, at under-17 level, and under-19 level. They are there for the benefit of one or two kids to try and get into your system. Whereas if you actually concentrate in developing all the players the cream will come to the top anyway. And that is where they pay for this kid coming out the SFA youth system, and it is then reinvested in the system to develop the next lot.

David Mackinnon

I firmly believe that in Scotland we still have an abundance of potentially great players and of course great coaches and managers. Today's economic situation mean though that clubs rarely take a chance on keeping late developers and many talented kids are lost to the game before they mature as adults and players. As General Manager and CEO the annual mantra from managers at contract time was "I'd love to keep him but we don't have the budget". Players with potential were cast aside with many disillusioned and subsequently lost to the game. I set up a company to take such kids. The US College system and the story of one is a lesson to be learned. A young 18 year old, 8 years at an SPL Club and Captain of the Youth team discarded not because of his football skill but because he was small and the Club felt they couldn't invest in him financially as he might never be able to cope with the physical side. The kid went to an American College and 4 years later at graduation was voted in the most valuable team at the MLS draft trials. As an industry we need to look after our players and coaches better than we currently do.

I believe we need to create the same educational system in the UK as in the USA albeit on a smaller scale to catch the potential stars of the future. This should be government funded and will either bring discarded players back into the game or create a wealth of motivated degree educated talent ready for industry.

The players generated via this scheme could provide a bank of talent which could be the nucleus of a lower league team in association with a local University and could provide players for sell on as well as attracting financial investment.

Jamie McGowan

I don't agree with it at all. I am not a fan of the SFA. I invested in it myself, got annoyed with it and that's it. I did a bit of coaching for Lanarkshire council, it was a waste of time and it was very robotic. They wanted to coach on how to defend, how to attack, I don't think that should happen anymore we should be having a holistic approach to the game.

Jackie McNamara

I am just not sure there is any scope for change.

A lot of people go on about how the SFA do their coaching. I just feel that everyone is doing the same thing and that is all they want when they are assessing you. I did my A licence in Ireland it was more a case of we are not sure of all the answers; but please explain how and why you are doing certain things. I feel with the Scottish set-up in a similar situations we are not as procative.We need to be far more open to new suggestions.

Darren Jackson

Having talked about all the problems we need to find solutions and unless we do radically change the way we think about how we develop young players then too much is left to chance. I like the concept of giving players other chances as not everybody develops physically or mentally at the same time. The more flexible our approach and the better links to alternative education paths the better for players at both the top and bottom of our game.

It is not something that I can see working here in Scotland. There are too many other things that need to change way before anything a radical as this has a chance of working.

Sandy Clark

I'm not sure that it is feasible in this country. How would the SFA decide who they are taking them under the umbrella and then how do they distribute them to wherever? I know there is still the gold, silver and bronze scheme and if you invest in so much in coaches and developing players you get a set amount of money so would they get first pick?

So, by that stage they have to be developed as players so say they did at 17. The infrastructure is not there at school which would be in our case, the coaching, the development, the sports science and the monitoring that it takes.

I still think that players come through and find their level. You will get the late developers, you get those at 15, 16 who look brilliant but end up playing at a lower level because they haven't quite made it.

CONCLUSION

I started thinking about how radical we could be and of course I didn't really expect our experts to go for it. What does strike me is that in discussion with them they all to a man recognise the fact that Scottish football needs a radical overhaul from all parts of the game. I think the main word to emphasis here is RADICAL as we have probably reached the nadir / watershed moment and that everything needs to be on the table and worked through. The difficulty for our experts is that just as fans don't have a proper voice (you know I will be doing my bit to try to change that) nor do players or manager and coaches and until that changes it will be difficult to go forward. In England the National St.George's Football Academy has just launched - should we have the same here? Probably, but how will it be funded? We also need to start looking at how we can improve the game from the bottom up as well as from the top down. Why is it when I was at Stirling Albion we trained two nights a week and yet one of our female fans who played for Rangers Ladies was training on four nights . There has got to be a way that we can look again to Scandinavia to see where they have flexible working after training every morning. We also need to be considering a professional exit strategy with proper links to the scholarship system and to junior clubs.

15 CLUB PARTNERSHIPS RAISE THE STANDARD

The loaning of players has long been a thorny issue in the world of football, whether it is from the point of view of the parent club who lets a player leave on loan and while they are there, they suffer an injury (which can potentially prevent teams from potential sales through transfers in the long run) or not being able to recall a player after an injury crisis.

Since the collapse of the SPL reserve league at the end of the 2008/09 season, Scottish football has faced a dilemma in how to get the best young players game time. Many teams focused on organising friendlies, specifically with English opponents in the aftermath of the cancellation of the league. The standards of these games overall was decent but like most friendly games, the tempo was not ideal and the extra travelling did not help. If young players are not being offered an environment to thrive in a competitive league structure, then they surely must be exposed to competitive football at some level.

A loan system where clubs can potentially have access up to six players from a club is one idea that could be possibly looked at. That would be the maximum but if there was opportunities for top-flight sides to allow young players experience to see if they can cope with league football.

It goes without saying that young SPL talents are regularly going on loan to Scottish Football League teams but I believe it could be a great thing if there was a system put in place, which guaranteed a certain number of young players game time in the SPL.

For example an SPL team would be able to get several talented players real game experience at a club and if it proved successful there would be an opportunity to field more youngsters in the seasons that would follow.

Example - If three SPL players spent a season on loan at an SFL division two club, you would be bringing in players who are already familiar with each other and could help each during their season on loan. You would end up with three alternatives at the end of the season

a) A player who is good enough to make an impact at parent club or similar level

b) A player who is probably not quite of SPL standard but has potential for career in football at some level

c) A player who is probably not capable of making a career in football long-term

Recently I had a conversation with a highly successful Scottish manager and he said one of the biggest problems when young players from his club were going out on loan to lower league sides was that they thought they had already made it. This seems to be a problem that other Scottish managers have encountered when big team youngsters arrive at their club. There is a feeling that certain youngsters are not pleased to be dropping divisions and in the process are not getting the most out of the opportunity.

If a loan structure was put in place, it would allow young players to come to terms with the notion that going out on loan is part of their development. If young players begin to relish going out on loan then the system of SPL-SFL player deals could thrive in the long run. It has to be viewed as an opportunity to thrive rather than viewing it as a punishment.

For a long time it has been mooted that SPL sides, specifically Old Firm duo Celtic and Rangers, were interested in the potential of allowing their reserve side (Under-21s) to compete in the lower leagues. Discussions have taken place but there was never any concrete plans for the possibility of change.

The idea of having youth sides competing in a country's league structure is not a new idea; it has been used for many years in Spain. The top youth sides (B teams) in Spain are able to be promoted/relegated between the second tier (Segunda Division) and the bottom tier (Tercera Division, 18 league Pyramid system) of the league structure.

One of the most interesting aspects is the 'B' teams are solely reliant on their own performances. The results of the 'A' have no bearing on what league they play in. Some of the most successful teams in recent seasons have been Real Betis B, Real Zaragoza B and Villarreal B.

In this next section I take a look at how the B team system has affected one Spanish club more than most.

A and B spells trouble

As of the 2012/13 season, only two B teams are currently competing in the Segunda Division and it probably doesn't surprise you that those teams are Barcelona B and Real Madrid Castilla; however that doesn't tell the whole story of B team success in the Spanish league.

Villarreal are a club who have performed wonders in recent years. In the 2005/06 season the 'Yellow Submarines' reached the UEFA Champions League semi-final, a remarkable achievement for a club who play in a town smaller than six of their La Liga rivals stadia.

The club had been one of the top teams in Spain for the last half decade; most of their success was down to their excellent youth policy, shrewd signings and tactical knowledge of Chilean coach Mauricio Pellegrini. The club had begun to slip to mid table after Pellegrini left for Real Madrid but no one could envision the developments during the 2011/12 season.

After losing star player Santi Cazorla to newly-rich Malaga, things went from bad to worse when goal machine Giuseppe Rossi was sidelined for the rest of the season when he ruptured his anterior cruciate against Real Madrid.

Suddenly Villareal found themselves in dire straits and even though by mid-April it had looked that they may just avoid relegation, their fate was confirmed on the final day after a 1-0 defeat against Atletico Madrid, their rollercoaster of defying the odds was over, and Villarreal were now a Segunda Division side.

That relegation didn't't just affect the 'A' team it had ramifications for the 'B' side as well. Villarreal B up until last season had competed admirably in Spain's second tier but the knock on effect of Villarreal's relegation meant the side also had to drop down a division to Segunda Division B. The B team finished a comfortable 12th in the 2011/12 campaign. For a club like Villarreal, who had been accustomed to attracting high calibre players this has been a body blow which effects their football operations from top to bottom.

After looking at the case of Villarreal, you cannot help but wonder what would have been if a Rangers 'B' had been in the SFL league system when the club went in to liquidation. It would have certainly muddied the waters in terms of where the club ended up playing their football this season.

There is an argument to be made for B teams potentially being involved in the league structure but I believe that there is real potential in a dedicated loan system agreement between SPL and SFL clubs in the future. There are many potential scenarios but I believe if an SPL club deals with an SFL club exclusively it would help in the long term.

Another area that remains under exploited is in the development of relationships with foreign clubs. As yet nobody has been able to create a platform that would successfully work for both clubs.

for it

- it helps clubs loaning players to get game time
- it helps player development with meaningful development

- colt teams could be attractive to crowds
- colt teams would help bigger clubs

against it

- often depends on the players attitude to being loaned
- colt teams could stop the pyramid
- colt teams could give some teams competitive advantage

WHAT OUR EXPERTS THINK:

Donald McGruther

Not really an area I can offer an opinion on except to say that I think lots of players have used the loan system well to get their careers to go in the right direction. Charlie Adam did a great job for St Mirren in their promotion season and went back to Rangers and on to the Premier League and Internationals.

Bryan Jackson

As long as the structure of any loan agreement works for both clubs then it should be allowed to evolve as part of making the whole game better.

Jocky Scott

I think the way it currently operates between Premier League clubs and lower league sides is that you have to have a working relationship with the manager who is already in place. In the past when I have loaned players to another club there has been at least part payment of the players wages. And the higher up the league you go, their players are earning more than the other players in the league. Therefore they are looking for a return, then it comes back to the point about have relationships with your peers.

As a manager I would want them to go somewhere where I know they are going to get looked after and that they are playing at a decent standard of team. You want to know that are going to learn because the manager or coach is of a high standard. There are plenty of positives regarding getting young players out on loan. The worry is that if you have them out on loan at a club that is struggling you are unsure of how much they are actually learning in a situation like that.

It is a great idea having players out on loan, if a part-time club is able to get a subsidised full-time player at the club. It is good for them if they can get a player from a full-time club because 9 times out of 10 they are getting a better standard of player coming into the club, or if it is a kid, he should be eager to impress. He will come on, and he will want to play and learn which will help in from an experience point of view. As the manager of the full time team, you know who is playing a better level than the under-19 league.

John Blackley

I think there is no doubt like many things it could be improved but for me it will always come down to the relationship between the two managers at each of the clubs and of course the attitude of the player who has to want it.

Steven Tweed

I think there is little chance of B teams happening. Obviously the Old Firm would want them and the Edinburgh clubs and probably Aberdeen and Dundee Utd too. Maybe if as part of league reconstruction it will be looked at as a way of supporting regionalised leagues. As far as the loan system I think it probably works ok at the moment.

Davie Hay

I am sure Celtic and Rangers would jump at the chance to develop players with a B team but I am not sure how many we could accommodate or if other clubs would vote for it. As far as the loan system goes I can't see many advantages in formalising it any anyway. You only send boys to managers you trust.

Kevin McGoldrick

If young SPL players can go and play second division against experienced players I think it could help their development greatly. I think if you can bring players in that can help the team then it is a good idea. I don't think supporters are too fussed, as long as the team is winning games and winning titles then I don't think it really matters if it loan players who are contributing, a lot of established Scottish player have made their name in the past after enjoying a loan spell at lower division club.

Alex Smith

Maybe it would be a concession to Celtic and Rangers to have colt teams in D3 as it would help bring in bigger crowds and help them develop talent at our two biggest academies. As for the loan system I think it works reasonably well as it stands.

Des McKeown

I hope you that you still get players that will continue to play their career with one club, or across two or three clubs. Look at Stephen Craigan, he has just retired after four years at Partick Thistle and then twelve years at Motherwell. The main problem with loan deals has been the club that is loaning out the player, too often it is trying to get someone off the wage bill, it has not about the development of players.. For me that fails before it even starts because managers will only put out players to clubs where they think they can be coached in the right manner.

I think it comes back to the point about nationalising the youth system. The SFL look after them until they are up to the age of 16. They develop it, because I can tell you Celtic are spending £1.6m a year on a youth system for what? James Forrest comes through, granted but is that enough? Celtic release almost a full squad of 19s every single season. It would be more economical to spend £400k on the best four kids in Scottish football, £100k for each of the best youngsters in the country. They could start in the lower leagues and then move up, instead of the other way around.

David Mackinnon

A solid idea which would enhance the experience of loaned players as well as providing improved standards at lower levels.

Jamie McGowan

Like most things it is something that could no doubt be improved. It is good for small clubs to see potential stars of the future and of course it helps their development as players.

Jackie McNamara

At Partick Thistle, I took four players on loan last season. Some were excellent with the right attitude and another who just thought he would come to the club and be the best player and didn't need to work for it. Yet we had our own kids there who were desperate, they might not quite have the same level of ability; but they had the desire and hunger and work ethic and in a situation like that I am stopping them having the opportunity to compete for a place.

At our club we haven't had it structured properly. We had bodies, to fit a criteria of the Under 19s, the coaching wasn't there, now we have tried to put in place where one of my senior players looks after them in the reserves and we have a couple of 16 year olds, 17 year olds and a couple 19 year olds at that age group and they are getting taught rather than just training to fit a criteria that is getting money from the club. I think that you were getting, £45,000 or something like that for the whole structure where the SPL clubs were getting £110,000 and a £145,000 from the SFA. It's all box ticking, it's what it has always been about box ticking, I believe that if they do not want us to have a good youth system in place, the bigger clubs would rather just cherry pick our best players who have made it in the first-team.

Darren Jackson

I think it is good that we look at all the options and talk to everybody involved in the process to see if we can be improved. I have no doubt that there could be ways that we can make it better if we evaluated it properly.

Sandy Clark

I think the loan system is fine the way it is. It can work for both sides if the relationship is good between the clubs and managers involved. Players move on now because of freedom of contract. Very rarely does anyone spend more than three or four years at one club but it is important that young players get the opportunity to go and play at a competitive level.

Conclusion

The colt team concept has been looked over the past few years and could have some merit for the teams that can afford them bringing a bit of glamour and excitement to far flung places such as Stranraer and Peterhead if the bottom league were extended as per Alex Smith's suggestion otherwise it would not attract much support from the smaller clubs. The loan system seems to be working ok and is not in need of any major changes according to the professional experts.

16 FINANCIAL CONTROLS - IF YOU CHEAT YOU ARE PUNISHED

Real businesses really can't cheat for very long. In recent times we have had a whole list of clubs in Scotland who have failed to live within their means. In simple terms that means hurting people and we are not just talking about the tax man. Livingston failed to pay the Council, and literally dozens upon dozens of businesses were hit by the failures at Dundee and Rangers

David Gold ex owner of Birmingham City and current owner of West Ham United said in 2010, "We almost need saving from ourselves. The greatest driving factor is the overall requirement to succeed or avoid relegation, so clubs take risks". This is probably one of the most striking and truthful comments from any club chairman.

In recent years all clubs must operate in the black. If they do not directors fail the fit and proper test and SFA representation is suspended until it is corrected. Well that seems to be the theory anyway.

The so-called football-creditor rule has long been controversial, since debts not only to competitor clubs but also to millionaire players are repaid in full in the event of the collapse of the football league or Premier League club. By contrast small creditors in the local community, often including schools and charities like the St John Ambulance, are paid a fraction of their dues when the club emerges from administration through a company voluntary arrangement (CVA). Whilst in Scotland we don't have the football creditor rule, remember all the players made redundant at clubs such as Motherwell and Dundee in recent times got the same CVA deal as everybody else it still is wrong that clubs can run up debt usually to the tax man and just expect to pay a small proportion of it. For far too long other businesses are decried and when it comes to football it is deemed to be acceptable because of the important connection to the community.

In court, Gregory Mitchell, QC, for HMRC, described the football creditors' rule as the "ugly side of the beautiful game". Arguing why it should be scrapped he explained: "Insolvency is a very real hazard in the football league.

"As a result of the operation of the (football creditor) rule all of the football creditors are paid in full while others who are unsecured receive, if they're lucky, a small dividend if anything at all. "We say these rules are contrary to the fundamental principles of insolvency laws and are void."

"Football clubs are substantial businesses – when a football club becomes insolvent there is a long list of businesses whose interests are prejudiced by the rules."

Mitchell also added there had been 36 football insolvencies since 2002; the FL effectively argues the current arrangement is designed to give protection to financially well-managed clubs against the risk of other sides being unable to meet their financial obligations.

It insists the system is necessary to protect the integrity of its competitions in circumstances where clubs, not only play against each other, but also conduct business.

A spokesman for HMRC said: "We are satisfied that the whole issue of the football creditors' rule has been fully aired in court."

The Football League declined to comment.

However in late April Greg Clarke, the chairman of the Football League, announced new financial fair play rules which he believed will lead to a more stable future for the Football League. From a Scottish perspective I expect these rules will be looked at very closely as we seek to re constitute our league post the David Murray and Craig Whyte debacle at Ibrox. I don't pretend to know a lot about this complex area but I do know that in the case of Rangers to continue playing they had to assume the football debts of the old company and so whilst Hearts, Dundee Utd and Austria Vienna will be paid, the guy who does some painting for them or had their taxi account won't.

Greg Clarke, the chairman of the Football League, said when discussing the new rules that his clubs had agree to abide by:

"I'd like to commend the Championship clubs for the courageous decision they have taken today. It means that for the first time, all 72 Football League clubs have agreed to take concerted action towards controlling their financial destiny.

"Whilst we cannot promise that these rules will deliver results overnight, they will begin to lay the foundations for a league of financially self-sustaining football clubs."

In simple terms it demands that new rules mean that clubs will be required to provide a set of accounts to the Football League by 1 December each year highlighting whether they have stayed within limits on loss-making and shareholder equity investment.

Championship clubs will see permitted losses drop from an acceptable deviation of £4m in 2011-12 to £2m by 2015-16. The permitted level of shareholder equity investment will reduce from £8m for 2011-12 to £3m by 2015-16.

Sanctions for failure to meet these guidelines depend on whether the club was promoted, remained in the Championship or was relegated. In the case of promotion, the club would have to pay a "Fair Play Tax" on the excess by which they failed to fulfill the fair play requirement, ranging from 1% on the first £100,000 to 100% on anything over £10m.

Any proceeds will be distributed equally among those clubs who complied with the regulations for the season in question. Clubs failing to meet the criteria but who remain in the Championship will be subject to a transfer embargo. Any side relegated from the Premier League will not be subject to sanctions in their first season in the Championship, as long as they have met their financial obligations under Premier League regulations. There will be a transition period before the system is fully embedded in the Football League culture.

So we can see that our colleagues across the border are taking this issue very seriously indeed and in a Scottish context it is essential that similar binding regulations are in place that has a similar effect. What is also essential is that ALL the clubs and the general public know what will happen with a certain set of circumstances well in advance rather than speculating or trying to do deals to suit vested interests.

Areas that should be explored by a financial working party include
- Fit and proper test making it effective
- Financial regulation by authorities
- Salary capping
- Annual audits
- % of wages to turnover agreement
- Administration avoidance plans (e.g. we all know that Kilmarnock has debts of £9m so what is happening to change that situation)

For it
- better regulation will benefit football
- fairer distribution of wealth means more competitive leagues

Against it
- there is only so much that the authorities can do to investigate properly - which is no excuse for not trying

WHAT OUR EXPERTS THINK:

Donald McGruther

I guess this is the why you asked me to contribute. I have been asked several times to step into rescue clubs when it all goes wrong and it is never pleasant and you always feel for the fans. Aside of the obvious problem of money being spent where there was none and debts being accumulated or hidden, it all it sadly comes down to the people in charge and them just not doing what they should be doing. The rules have been too lax and the fact they have started to look at this in Europe should wake us up to the fact that we need to be changing here in Scotland. I don't know what we are waiting for.

Bryan Jackson

I could write a book about this in itself. We need to be realistic and realise that the football authorities will always find it difficult to ensure that the "right people" get into football clubs. The due diligence process is difficult and unless the owners come forward and admit to serious breaches it is hard to police. I think like many people do that the rules of engagement have changed and need to be completely rewritten. Whilst it may be difficult to implement, standard breaches should be met with a set tariff. Some sort of due diligence needs to be done before new owners arrive and existing owners need to show regular financial competence.

Jocky Scott

One of the biggest problems with regards to that is that the Premier League have their own rules, whereas the football league don't have any rules with regards to administration. That was proved with regards to Livingston, when they went into administration, they got put down two leagues and had to start again, Dundee got deducted 25 points and a fine – they were both into administration; nothing was different between that. It was two different clubs, why did one club get punished one way and the other club another way? Because the football league didn't have a ruling. They just decided at that particular point in time, we will do away with Livingston whereas Dundee were a bigger club we will dock them 25 points and give them a fine. The one at Dundee was simply because one individual said he would carry the costs of the club for two years, where after 8 months he decided he wasn't doing that. So there was nobody to pay tax bills or nobody to pay wages.

Well, the fans when the club went into administration were saying we can't let our club go down. They were out with the buckets at the home games, travelled in their numbers to away games. That was great for the club, but for the team the backing that the supporters gave them when for 90 minutes they never got on the players backs. They cheered them when they made mistakes, cheered when the ball went out the park...they cheered them when they missed a goal, cheers them when they lost a goal and went 1-0 down. Now before administration, any of these things they would be right on top of the player because of the expectation "we are a big club in the first division, we should be winning". It was no coincidence that in that period that Dundee went 17 or 18 games undefeated, and the players played with freedom that wasn't there before administration.

John Blackley

In my view this is why we have the league and SFA. Surely that are the custodians of the game and should make sure that everything possible is being done to stop clubs overspending, stop these rogue owners coming in to the game and making sure the club remains in a healthy condition. I just don't think they take this aspect of the job seriously which is to the detriment of the game.

Steven Tweed

I think there have to be financial regulations which allow a club to finish a season. There should be a structure where if clubs go into administration during the season, they have to get the books up front early on to know that they are going to fulfil their commitments to their salaries and the leagues. We have to take this aspects of our game seriously and let's be honest we have been let down by Hampden on this.

Davie Hay

We don't look very clever when we see what has been happening under the noses of the football authorities and nothing is done about it. It is essential that football survives and that we get back to football people running it and making decisions based on what is best for the game. We need regulations that work and administrators who know what they are doing.

Kevin McGoldrick

I don't claim to know much about the business side of football but I think it is plain to see that the rules need to be tightened up. Things that happen in football would just not happen in any normal business and I think there is far too much politics being played rather than thinking about our game.

Alex Smith

There is so much that needs changed and we need to start with looking at how we govern the game and who governs the game. I just can't see how we can continue to ignore the fact that this mess was allowed to happen. Is it true that the people in power at the leagues were really powerless? I don't think so. We need to refresh all the rules and ensure that everybody plays according to those rules and if they don't then they know the consequences they face.

Des McKeown

We often hear about the game being brought into disrepute by a player or manager or most recently a Chairman and they are jumped on by the football authorities. The fiasco we have had in recent months has brought unprecedented damage to our game and I would argue the actions of many have brought it into disrepute - so where is the punishment? I have no faith that anything will change.

David Mackinnon

Yes but more governance rules must be introduced as the current SFA and SPL regulations are totally inadequate and were clearly exposed as such during the Rangers situation. Their "Fit and Proper" rules are not followed through to any great extent and as a result in my opinion the prospect of an individual or group taking over a club and running it into the ground still exists.

Jamie McGowan

We have had enough of cheating - buying players you can't afford and not living within your means and this is just the ones we hear about. The football authorities should make this their priority seeing who comes into our game and ensuring that they work within the rules.

Darren Jackson

It kind of goes without saying that we need to be better at this. Clubs having massive debts is not healthy for the game nor is us having owners who don't have the right credentials. Hopefully this is an area that is being tightened by the authorities after this summer's events.

Jackie McNamara

I think that this is where the administrators should be taking a look at themselves as they presided over the mess. In four years we have seen Gretna, Livingston, Dundee and now Rangers all fall over. The rules need to be tougher and they need to be adhered to at the end of the day we cannot cheat on the park, so why should it be allowed off the park?

Sandy Clark

First and foremost you shouldn't cheat. If you do cheat, you should pay a price. Unfortunately the goal posts have moved depending on who the club are for obvious reasons. Everyone has to be aware of the rules of the industry there are in. In football terms, it has happened in the past. I think you would have to take every case on its own merit. Is it bad luck? If it is deliberate obviously it is more serious. Bottom line is if there are discrepancies, then you have got to pay the price.

Football clubs in adversity will always come to the fore, I think the community thing ties in with it. I think it is worth noting that in football we live in a goldfish bowl. There are tons and tons of businesses that have gone into administration and people have pulled out of businesses and they have then folded.

I am a great believer in prudent spending in football. My chairman when I was at St Johnstone was a businessman and would say to me you cannot spend more than you make, it will not happen. If everybody does that, you are living within your means. If you get a windfall and you are progressing in the cup, you sell a player, great you get a bit more. But I think you should treat it like it's your own bank account. If you are earning £100 a week, don't be spending £200.

CONCLUSION

Footballs rules need updated and due diligence on any prospective owner of clubs is essential to ensure our clubs are in good hands. The football authorities need to ensure that financial fair play is in place and those who are breaking the rules are punished accordingly, preferably with punishments that are well published in advance. This is at the hub of good governance of our game.

17 GIVE FANS WHAT THEY WANT - ENTERTAINMENT AND EXCITEMENT

Fans are simple creatures of habit they want to see their team win (as often as possible) and they want to see theatre, drama, excitement - preferably on the park rather than off the park where far too much time and energy has been wasted in recent times.

There are elements of the game that have not evolved to allow the fans the excitement they want. How can we honestly think we can encourage existing customers (loyal fans) to stay and attract new customers (the vast majority of the public)

- Dump Challenge Cup recycle money down the pyramid replace with all clubs in League Cup with home and away ties in sections
- Experiment with the rules. Make it more fun attacking minded Dryburgh Cup example where a player can only be offside in an penalty box. Could the Ramsden Cup be the place where we experiment a bit and got back to UEFA and FIFA with research findings. (games with no offside, sin bins rather than yellow cards, kick ins rather than throw ins, trainers on the park while the game goes on, additional roles for4th official etc etc) This would make it interesting for fans and start to get us innovating again.
- Cross Border competition like the old Anglo Scottish Cup, maybe close season rather than having random friendlies of low interest
- Scottish League Internationals brought excitement for league clubs. Could we bring it back in if the schedule is less crowded?
- Look at points system again (3 for an away win 2 for a home win 1 for a draw with potential 2 or 3 points after 0-0 draw with penalty shoot out)
- Under 19 or reserve team matches or ladies team matches on prior to main match, building our wider community audience and just doing something different!
- We already talked about a penalty shoot out if a game ended 0-0 (which is the least desirable outcome for fans). Occasionally we hear of 0-0 games being real crackers but unfortunately this is usually the exception so why not give both teams and incentive to get a winner in real time and if not then they can still have a chance to win it on penalties. Will keep all fans in the stadium to the very end and guarantee drama.

WHAT OUR EXPERTS THINK:

Donald McGruther

If we work on the basis that it is not very good entertainment now then yes we need to change it. I think we should be looking at rewarding what the fans want to see - so like more points for goals and making better rewards for winning away from home.

Bryan Jackson

I think that any business needs to keep evolving and there lies the problem with football as it has been a market that has stagnated. But like many things in Scottish football, nobody has managed to come forward to implement any positive plans and the old adage in business is that if you are not going forward then you are actually going backwards.

Jocky Scott

Remember we tried the no offside to the penalty box in the Dryburgh cup? Well, unfortunately right now the offside rule is a joke. The way that it is nobody knows how it works. Players don't know if the opposition are onside or offside or whatever. As coaches, you hone the skill of when to come out and play offside and you teach them when to sit back and not play offside, and you see teams now stepping up and not fully sure of what they should be doing. And there are three players standing offside, but the one who has scored is apparently onside. In our day, if you were in an offside position, you were offside. Regardless if the ball was heading to the player or not, you were offside and the linesman just kept going (gestures of raising a flag). Everyone knew, players fans – and now...nobody knows.

John Blackley

I like the idea of making it more entertaining but as long as we don't interfere with the fundamentals of the game that we all love. Ok you can argue that it has been too slow to evolve if you just take the example of goal line technology with tennis and rugby taking their sports on to be even more professional. I quite like the idea you had about making 0-0 draws a thing of the past with penalties at the end of the game to make it more exciting. Things like that that don't actually alter the rules are worth considering.

Steven Tweed

Rugby is maybe different; it went from part-time to full time, it was a bit easier to incorporate some of that at the start. This is something that has been going on for a long time. You don't just pick it up and change it overnight. And maybe there is something, at the end of the season you get extra bonuses

Davie Hay

I think it all stems from Americanisation of sport where they never have draws. I think rugby now gives you extra points for doing different things. I tend to think that people are scared about change for change sake. In my day as a player, I lost a game on a coin toss, that is hardly fair but I remember people at the time saying penalties wouldn't work but they are probably the fairest way to do it and they are very exciting. Football should always be open to change.

Kevin McGoldrick

I think we need to be rewarding players and teams who entertain. It might work well in the three divisions below the SPL; but with Celtic and Rangers there is too big a gulf between their resources than the others so incentivising them to score more or giving them extra points etc will just not work.

Alex Smith

We need to think about the whole game as a package not just in little bits. Attendances have been falling for years but we have never come up with a plan to get punters back into the game. Not only do we not have fair competition in the top leagues but we also are competing against the weather, other sports and of course now the Premier League in England and La Liga in Spain. If we want to be second or third rate then fine but I believe in Scottish football and I think we are better than that.

Des McKeown

GOALS GOAL GOALS that is what the punters want. They say, always give the striker the benefit of the doubt. I'm quite happy knowing there is a striker in there because he has been lazy, and then the ball has been played and he is still in there and he is not offside...that's wrong.

I think you should incentivise clubs. Incentivise for more goals scored or having a better difference between for and against. Certainly I think there are no draws in any American sports; Their fans expect a game to be won.

I wouldn't change the rules to any huge degree, I think the offside one can be confusing for a lot of people and I think purely from a selfish point of view, I preferred it when you knew. I worked my backside off to get out of the box and if a lazy striker is sat in there he shouldn't get the benefit of the rule change.

David Mackinnon

Let's not re-invent the wheel, look at the best options available in leagues throughout the world and bring best practice to our game. One thing though, please ask the fans what they think. Despite many loud voices saying we must seek the thoughts of the fans it never happens.

What successful business operates in a vacuum with seeking the input from their customers? Oh yes Scottish Football.......

Jamie McGowan

I would like to see it incentivised for winning away from home. Other teams go and sit, and if it's the last 20 minutes. But if you get more points for it...I think it would be a great idea.

Jackie McNamara

I think that comes down to league structure. There is a fear element. In our league there are a few teams that will not come out, won't even try to play football, they will just smash the ball into the corner.

But there is other games we have played better and came away with nothing. It is just football sometimes.

I think the league needs to be different. There is a fear in the league definitely. There is a fear of losing, its right through not just in our league but in the top league as well. It is all geared to stop, rather than to go and score. They will stop the other team from playing, then put four strikers on in the last 20 minutes and say that they had a go.

I don't think that you come up with a punishment or a mechanism for it, I think that if the leagues change – it will change because there is less fear. Obviously there will be teams near the bottom that will still play that way as they will need to come and get something but it will come a problem if they are going to win things, just not to sit and defend.

As far as offside is concerned it is not working. Change it back to what it was before, there is no confusion or grey areas. If you are offside you are offside - interfering or not. Changes have single handily stopped teams from playing the offside trap. The offside trap was a great skill that clubs could do if they were well drilled. Who does it anymore, you very rarely see a team doing it anymore. There is too much doubt now.

I don't think the goals are the problem, surely it is trying to encourage teams to come out and attack away from home. There are some teams that have the same mentality, regardless of where they play they are going out to win. But my God there are some teams which have a totally different attitude when then go and play away from home. You know, Kenny Shields got a fair bit of stick for having a dig at Ayr United in the semi-final of the League Cup and in a way he was right as Ayr had one shot on goal after 86 minutes.

I remember when Craig Levein went to Dundee United, and I think they got beat by seven at Ibrox, and he said "We were getting a chasing; but there was a time when we were 3-0 with 20 minutes to go and as a player I would always try and make sure we would keep it at three". You make a very good point when they did change the win from 2 points to 3 points there was an outcry, two points for a win one point for a draw was how it always had been.

No, I am just saying you might be right but my perception is more that teams play away from home and sit in, we hear that expression "playing on the counter" and don't try and win, and do you know what? There are two lots of supporters that are there to be entertained, and I would argue that if you turned around and said no point for a home draw for example, 1 point for an away draw, 2 points for a home win and 3 points for an away win, something like that where you would see an extra reward. The only time you can get three points is when you win away from home and then you would get hopefully, every team going for it when they played away from home. There are managers who will still try and think of a loop hole to and do what they always do and strangle the game for 89 minutes and try to get a set piece.

Darren Jackson

It would be good to see us try to get more people into the stadiums on a regular basis as it has a huge impact on the players performance having a great atmosphere in the stadiums. I think the fundamentals are all there but we just need to start talking the game up and of course making the structures work for us rather than holding us back.

Sandy Clark

I don't know how you could bring changes for extra points for goals. You could trial it in the lowest division? The extra point for scoring 5 goals. I don't think you would ever get the extra point for a defender scoring a goal as they would all be registered as defenders at the start of the season. But I think something like more points for 3 goals or 4 goals potentially.

Say it was 0-0, have a penalty shoot-out then the winning team gets 1 point and the losing side gets no points. Something like that is worth trying, and might make it more exciting. Does it mean they will go for it from the start as they know that nothing might be in it for them?

I think the offside discussion is a tricky one. I don't know about the phases, second phases or all; but I preferred the old offside rule that we all played with and knew. You have to be aware defensively of everyone in the pitch. I am not sure that if a player is standing offside then another runs through and he is not offside, but then cuts it back. I am not sure that is correct, but it seems to be how a lot of goals are scored today.

CONCLUSION

Are there things that we can do we do that make the game more exciting and different? Can we do away with points for a non scoring draw with a penalty shoot out for all the points. Could we reintroduce the Anglo Scottish Cup to replace Ramsden Cup which would create better value for fans and the sponsors? Give me a white board and a few hours and we can come up with dozens of these suggestions. Of course many of these will only truly work if we embrace bigger changes in the game such as league reconstruction and getting fairer competition etc. However, any business that does not go forward is going backwards. Let's at the very least try things that don't necessarily alter the rules in any significant ways.

18 GROUND SHARING AND SWEATING THE ASSET

The biggest cost apart from wages that any club faces is its stadium (and its upkeep) and of course we all know that the stadiums by their nature are pretty much white elephants. They were never designed to do much else apart from play football. In the past of course it was different. I am old enough to remember when Clyde played at Shawfield which was also home to Greyhound Racing and the Glasgow Tigers Speedway. If only they had a little bit of Barcelona vision and bought into these other sports that could potentially be used to make the ground a more valuable asset.

A generation before I can recall my Dad telling me about watching athletics, boxing and I am sure they even tried speedway at Firhill or was it Greyhound Racing, I can't quite remember. More recently the Glasgow Warriors did great things for the Thistle coffers; but it meant the park was a nightmare to play on. Of course we have had Cowdenbeath with stock car racing, but the less said about the stadium the better. The big issue is that unless you have the space and cash to maybe put a hotel in next to the stadium (it worked at Kilmarnock - although they managed to accumulate around £5m of debt to get there) there is little else you can do to maximise the value of the asset. Of course further down the league we see the likes of Alloa Athletic, Stenhousemuir and Montrose starting to make significant profits from using the latest technology available to them to get 3 and 4 G parks down that they can rent out. Aside of the odd concert (Elton John at Falkirk this close season) there remains little a club can do to get more revenue from its biggest fixed asset. Although I believe several clubs are using their functions suites during the week catering for funerals and why not - if you can't bring them into the ground when they are alive then at least you are generating some cash from the lucrative market of folk being dead!

Ground sharing of course could bring significant economic benefits as the cost of running the stadium is halved. With a shared stadium there would be a real feel of community and you would hope stronger benefits going back to areas of operation. Hopefully there could also be environmental benefits in getting rid of old dilapidated inefficient buildings and replacing them with new stadium structures. Surely there has got to be a deal done in Dundee where Dens Park is owned by a Dundee Untied Director? Time for a chat about the future?

<u>*WHAT OUR EXPERTS THINK:*</u>

Donald McGruther

Should have been done years ago but too many vested interests mean it will never happen.

Bryan Jackson

From a financial prospective, it is obvious that there should be ground sharing and making as much as you can of your stadium. However, it is football and the nature of most fans and clubs means that it is unlikely that it will happen. The situation in Dundee is probably the most obvious example but you still cannot really ever imagine the two clubs sharing.

Jocky Scott

Too many stadiums now been redeveloped so I can't see it happening now.

John Blackley

I think it would only have happened if we had won the Euro Championship hosting that we tried for a few years back. I think it had proposals for a new Dundee stadium and a new one in Aberdeen

Steven Tweed

It could be quite hard given the geography but I think everybody has to be looking at anything like this that could take the game forward.

Davie Hay

If it can work in big clubs in Spain and Italy then why not here. The obvious one is Dundee; but I am sure there are others that it would work for.

Kevin McGoldrick

Apart from the Dundee scenario it is hard to think of any other alternatives. Clubs if they had been open to it could have thought it through. I was thinking about a combined site between Greenock and Paisley could have suited both clubs when Love Street was sold.

Alex Smith

We don't have enough people watching the games and with big stadiums empty then it makes perfect sense to do it. What we have seen over the years is clubs not thinking big. So when East Fife were building a new stadium why not put it nearer Kirkcaldy and them and Raith could share as they are just about 12 miles apart.

Des McKeown

So obvious and I think it is all about getting the best use of the limited assets that we have. As long as it is not rugby - look what happened to Thistle when they had Glasgow Warriors there - shocking surface for playing football but would Jackie prefer that or the extra money it brought to build his squad?

David Mackinnon

A firm yes, but owned by the local council and used 7 days a week by the community. Ronnie Macdonald has undertaken an amazing job at Hamilton utilising the stadium to its full with a close partnership with the Council. A stadium can be the heart and soul of the community but only if a clear buy in is established by all partners. Any ground-sharing plan should be well planned and ensure not only match day expenditure is shared as a result but that the stadium is utilised fully.

Jamie McGowan

Makes sense we could have a central belt hub with all the clubs such as Stirling Albion, Falkirk, Stenhousemuir, Alloa, East Stirling all playing games at say the two best stadiums. Forthbank and the Falkirk stadium and maybe the other astro grounds being shared by the community and junior / amateur sides. We just need to think differently.

Jackie McNamara

I think that there are lost opportunities throughout the years and the most obvious one is Dundee. I thought it might happen when they last went into administration.

Darren Jackson

It is another one where history is against us. Apart from fans having issues with it I think there is just not enough opportunity to do it apart from probably Dundee which is just mad. Maybe a joint Edinburgh stadium would work depending on what might happen to Hearts as both are landlocked in areas of high density housing.

CONCLUSION

In many cases the opportunity has gone. With so little expansion left for the likes of

Tesco and Morrisions there are so few clubs left who will get that particular get out of jail free card. Using the stadiums and any other ways is problematic. At the big city level Dundee and Edinburgh are obvious opportunities waiting to be grasped but probably never will. Lower down the leagues getting off grass and onto Astro Turf make the clubs sustainable and gets them closer to the local community who can use the facility.

19 THE AFTER MATCH DISCUSSION

Supporters Direct Scotland, is the voice of football supporters' trusts in Scotland, and will in the coming years be publishing papers highlighting **what fans think** – key recommendations to shape the future of Scottish football. Below is what fans currently think based on the results of supporters' surveys over the past two years and a detailed analysis of the issues facing the game.

what fans think recommendations:

- *greater competition within Scottish league football structures*
- *equal funding for each team in a league*
- *support for clubs by central league management to increase the average attendance over a season of 20% by 2016, and achieve an average stadium capacity utilisation of 65% within 10 years*
- *two leagues of 16 teams, and a qualifying league of 10*
- *re-introducing the League Cup, with a mini-league qualifying format structured on a geographical basis with four teams in each group*
- *improved training and professional development for all players including greater use of Modern Apprenticeships and post-career planning*
- *the establishment and implementation of a strong club licensing scheme*

This data was compiled over two surveys and the main findings is that there remains a clear preference for larger leagues amongst Scottish football supporters (including Old Firm and other SPL supporters) Support for a 10/12 team top league has halved and is getting to the point where only those in the SPL offices in Hampden (and by default clubs in the league) want it.

This remains the case even when supporters are presented with the SPL's statement on the need for four Old Firm games to maintain broadcasting revenues. Fans feel that it is what they think as paying customers that should drive what the industry does not what Sky or ESPN say. If that means the clubs have less revenue then fine - they can spend less.

A 16 team league remains the most popular league size with supporters and there is broad support for a pyramid structure, a winter break and an earlier start to the season. Although support has risen for a summer season, opinion on this issue remains divided with a third of fans opposed to such a move. However hopefully by the time they have read this book that perception might just have changed.

Fair and reasonable competition is essential to our top league and strong support for distributing central revenues more equally and there is clear evidence that supporters believe this would increase competition. The benefits being that there are indications that increased competition would encourage greater attendance particularly amongst those who attend games less regularly and fans of clubs in the First Division and non Old Firm SPL clubs.

I am delighted to report (as it will make my job a lot easier) that there remains a very strong belief amongst supporters that they should be consulted on major issues that affect Scottish football.

The main priorities identified for being the need for the Scottish Football Network focused on representing fan opinion to the football authorities/Government and campaigning for improved rights for fans. That is why we launched www.scottishfans.org and the Fans Parliament in late October 2012. So please follow us on Facebook and on Twitter and get daily updates from our site.

What fans want in numbers (from 4000 plus respondents)
- 98% of fans believe that fans should be consulted on decisions to be taken about Scottish football
- 86% of fans want bigger leagues
- 83% of fans want a more equal distribution of central revenue
- 79% of fans want clubs to include fan representation on their board
- 72% of fans want a pyramid structure
- 63.5% of fans want an introduction of a winter break
- 59% of fans want an earlier start to the season in July
- 55% of fans want a summer season from March to November (summer football)
- 49% - If a 16 or 18 team approach is adopted for the top two leagues in Scotland then 49% of fans want to organise the remaining clubs in a regional league set up.

What fans want in summary (from 4000 plus respondents)
Ideas on how to improve Scottish football from fans include:
The main suggestions included the following (in order of mentions)

- A fairer distribution of the income in each league
- Larger leagues meaning less games making bigger games more special

- Play offs to the SPL every season
- Summer football
- Cheaper ticket prices
- Sectional League Cup
- Reserve league re-introduced
- Let the Old Firm leave if they want to leave
- Scottish/foreign player quotas
- Colt or Reserve teams in lower leagues
- A pyramid system
- Salary caps for players
- Reduce influence of TV (including cheaper pricing for live games)

CONCLUSION

Scottish Football is in a mess it needs radical change and some people with big ideas to step up to the plate if we are to not just get out of the mess, but start to grow again. The answers are all there and I believe that we need to listen to the Fans, the Players and the Coaches and Managers if we want the game to progress. For too long these voices have been ignored and as a result the whole game has suffered. If we rally round there is no better time for us all to contribute to Saving Scottish Football for future generations to enjoy. I hope to play my part in that through the development of www.scottishfans.org and Supporters Direct Scotland's model of building sustainable football clubs. I do hope that as I try to bring some of these campaigns off the pages and into life that you will support them. You as an ordinary fan have a huge role to play in this process and I do look forward to hearing your views too.

Saving Scottish football